Consumer Identity & Access Management:

Design Fundamentals

Simon Moffatt M.CIIS CISSP CCSP CEH

Contents

Prologue

Consumer identity and access management (CIAM) is a critical component of any modern organisation with digital services at its core. If you used the Internet yesterday, you would very likely have interacted with a website that had CIAM at its foundation.

Making an online purchase, checking a bank balance, getting a quote for car insurance, logging into a social media site or submitting and paying an income tax return. All of those interactions require high scale, secure identity and access management services.

But how are those systems designed? Today, organisations need to not only meet end user privacy, security and usability requirements, but also provide business enablement opportunities that are agile and can respond to market changes rapidly. The modern enterprise architect and CISO are no longer just focused upon internal employee security - they now need to address the growing demand for digital enablement across consumers and citizens too.

This book is primarily aimed at senior solution architects, enterprise architects and chief information security officers. They have between 3-7 years experience in analysing internal system architectures and are responsible for driving initiatives that deliver business value through the secure application of best practices. They will have a background in network, server and application infrastructure, with a basic grounding in security concepts.

The book is intended to be used as a conceptual and

foundational text, to provide a clear and concise grounding in the key challenges and design principles. Individual chapters would likely be referred to during specific parts of a project.

By the end of this book, the reader will understand:

- The key benefits and challenges of CIAM
- The requirements and design principles of a CIAM system
- The main technology components used in a CIAM system

And the reader will be able to:

- Analyse existing homegrown/legacy CIAM systems and recommend improvements
- Design new architectures for CIAM
- Make more informed vendor and system integration selections for CIAM projects

About the Author

Simon Moffatt is a recognised expert in the field of digital identity and access management, having spent nearly 20 years working in the sector, with experience gained in consultancies, startups, global vendors and within industry. He has contributed to identity and security standards for the likes of the National Institute of Standards and Technology[1] and the Internet Engineering Task Force[2].

[1] https://csrc.nist.gov/publications/detail/sp/800-204/final
[2] https://www.rfc-editor.org/rfc/rfc8628.txt

Simon is perhaps best well known as a public speaker and industry commentator via his site The Cyber Hut[3].

He is a CISSP, CCSP, CEH and CISA and has a collection of vendor related qualifications from the likes Microsoft, Novell and Cisco. He is an accepted full member of the Chartered Institute of Information Security (M.CIIS), a long time member of the British Computer Society and a senior member of the Information Systems Security Association. He is also a postgraduate student at Royal Holloway University, studying for a Masters of Science in Information Security.

Since 2013, he has worked at ForgeRock[4], a leading digital identity software platform provider, where he is currently Global Technical Product Management Director.

For more information see his home on the web[5].

Acknowledgements

This book has really been an accumulation of many years professional work and research in the field of identity management. From my first role working as a security administrator, through to more recently designing access management features for a software vendor, all of the roles, projects and colleagues I have worked under, alongside and lead have all contributed in some way to my experiences

3 https://www.thecyberhut.com
4 https://www.forgerock.com/
5 https://www.simonmoffatt.com

and in turn the content in these chapters.

Specific appreciation should go to those who have provided detailed feedback on the writing and content of this book, namely my many colleagues at ForgeRock and all the customers and perspectives I have worked with over the years. Specific "thank yous" are due to Neil Madden, Adam McElroy, Carlos Trigoso, Brad Tumy, Thomas Linke, Scott Forrester, Peter Strifas, John Pinson and Martin Sandren for detailed commentary and review on certain sections.

CHAPTER 1

What is CIAM?

If you used the Internet yesterday, you very likely interacted with a system that had the foundations based upon a consumer identity and access management (CIAM) system.

Making an online purchase, checking a bank balance, getting a quote for car insurance, logging into a social media site or submitting and paying your income tax return, all require high scale, secure consumer identity and access management services at their core.

But what are CIAM services? The initial point to consider, is for many, they are invisible. Like the electrical wiring in your home, you typically only acknowledge their existence, when they need repairing or replacing.

Yet, they are essential for the operation of essentially every online service that requires even the basic process of logging in.

CIAM is the key base component of delivering secure and personalised digital experiences on the modern web. It covers a myriad of use cases and capabilities, covering account creation, secure authentication and login, through to complex adaptive access, consent and data management, as it pertains to consumer information, in the age of "digital transformation"

Digital transformation (DX) is simply the "use of new, fast and frequently changing digital technology to solve problems."[6] We experience that new problem-solving capability daily and digital initiatives are driving efficiency, personalised experiences and revenue generation across both the public and private sectors.

Through the digital transformation journey, CIAM—estimated to be a ~$38 billion industry by 2023[7]—has become a key component of the chief information security officer's (CISO's) and enterprise architect's (EA's) portfolio of capabilities, that they often need to design, deliver and optimise.

Identity Evolution

Time Before Automation

Before we delve into the main theme of this chapter and discuss "What is CIAM?", let us first go back in time. Time before CIAM existed and indeed, time before automation was being applied to identity and access management (IAM) in general.

IAM itself is a term typically used to cover the management of employee centric accounts, permissions and associated workflows. It has evolved to become a complex set of

[6] https://en.wikipedia.org/wiki/Digital_transformation
[7] https://www.marketsandmarkets.com/Market-Reports/consumer-iam-market-87038588.html

mature capabilities that focus on the identity creation lifecycle and what that identity can do. We will cover IAM in more detail shortly.

If we take another step back in time, before IAM was itself a solution set, many IT systems performed rudimentary and typically very manual account management services. Siloed systems that did require a modicum of access control, often managed a local accounts database, that stored usernames and passwords. Each unique user was issued a username and associated password. The setup and management of those accounts was typically done manually–by a system administrator–often at the bequest of a line manager via a ticketing system.

Not all user accounts are created equally of course, and permissions were used to allow different user accounts to perform different tasks. Permissions are system specific capabilities, often managed via *groups*. A user would become a *member* of a group and the group would be associated with different access control lists that governed access to certain files or functions.

Manually upkeeping the creation and management of users, groups, permissions and passwords was highly error prone and inconsistent. Many operational inefficiencies existed, for both the system administrator and the end user.

Figure 1.1: Account management operational inefficiencies:

Cause	Effect
Inconsistent account naming standards	Account ownership difficult to map to real entity
Group descriptions missing or incomplete	User associated with incorrect groups, impacting security and usability
No group removal process	User moves job roles and accumulates entitlements
No user removal process	Employment termination results in orphaned accounts

Poor governance, standards and a lack of automation also created a cascading effort for the early day system user experience.

Figure 1.2: Account usage operational inefficiencies:

Cause	Effect
Inconsistently associated permissions	Borrowing and sharing of colleague accounts to perform job role
Disconnected system accounts	Having to remember multiple username and password combinations
Forgetting passwords	Time wasted on helpdesk reset

and being locked out of systems	calls

The lack of systemisation drove a wave of localised approaches to industrialising the account management lifecycle–from template based account and access request processes, workflows for password resets and approval processes for user to group changes.

Home grown automation however, gave way to the birth of multiple vendor supplied sub sectors within the entire identity and access management lifecycle.

Industrialization of IAM

The industrialization of employee focused identity and access management started in the 1990's with technologies such as centralised directories for storing user accounts and passwords, through to network operating systems that catered for the large scale sharing of files and data.

But first, let us break down the 'I' (identity) and 'A' (access) parts of IAM and the specific capability areas that started to develop. The 'I' is focused upon the creation and management of persistent user data, often stored within databases and directories.

Figure 1.3: Identity lifecycle high level capabilities:

Capability Area	Description

Centralised directory	Used to store user accounts
Access request system	Ability to request changes to permissions and entitlements
Approval workflow system	Line manager control over access requests
Access review system	Periodic retrospective validation of user entitlement associations
System audit tool sets	Provide system owners the ability to account misalignments
Synchronization & correlation engine	The linking of accounts in different systems for the bidirectional flow of data
Role based access control (RBAC) engineering	The automatic creation of roles based on business data (top down) and system entitlements (bottom up)
RBAC management	The governance and versioning of user to roles relationships

Rule based access control management	Use of HR data to associate users to roles via rules

Whilst the 'I' in IAM, is focused upon create, read, update and delete (CRUD) activities associated with user accounts, the 'A' is more focused upon runtime controls–typically *authentication* (who someone or something claims to be) and *authorization* (what they can do).

Figure 1.4: Access management high level capabilities:

Capability Area	Description
Central authentication service (CAS)	Ability to login using a single username and password using credentials from a central directory
Session management	Leverage the login process from a CAS to create time based access–expiry results in a relogin flow
Single sign on service (SSO)	Leverage the session created centrally to allow seamless login to multiple systems simultaneously
Authorization engine	Centralised policy engine that manages application specific task access

Enforcement agents	Software controllers that sit in front of protected applications and talk to the centralised authorization engine
Federation manager	Re-use a CAS from a trusted third party to allow access to locally protected systems
Multi-factor authentication (MFA)	Enhance the login process by using additional factors such as one time passwords (generated or sent via SMS/mail) or smart card possession
Contextual access manager	Analysis of non-identity data such as device, location, network and application to handle access control

The growth of the employee IAM market has been significant over the last 20 years—with numerous estimates suggesting in North America alone it represents a $10 billion opportunity[8].

With such a large—and continually growing[9]

[8]https://www.gminsights.com/industry-analysis/identity-and-access-management-market

[9]10% compound annual growth rate between 2019-2025—https://www.gminsights.com/industry-analysis/identity-and-access-management-market

sector—innovation by vendors and suppliers has been evident, with new emerging areas focused on leveraging machine learning for entitlements analysis, mobile behaviour analytics for improved authentication and the ever growing list of dedicated passwordless providers aiming to create a frictionless login.

So far we have discussed the emergence of the IAM field and some brief analysis of the capabilities many medium and large sized organisations have utilised. A final comment on IAM, is to focus upon the drivers of this sector. Why has it emerged as a multi-billion dollar market?

The inefficiencies described in *figure 1.1* and *figure 1.2* helped externalise home grown automation into a market delivering best of breed capabilities.

Figure 1.5: Example Drivers of employee IAM:

Driver	Origin	Example business benefit
Cost reduction	*Internal*—automation of the management of IT systems	Fewer personnel performing account administration tasks

Operational efficiency	*Internal*–centralised provisioning of account data	Reduced new employee onboarding time, resulting in increased productivity
Business enablement	*Internal*–user convenience from SSO, fewer password resets	Increased employee happiness and productivity
Compliance	*External*–adherence to industry regulation	Fewer data breaches, audit actions and fines
Risk Reduction	*Internal & External*–increased security via automated controls	Fewer data breaches, improved reputation

The birth of the employee focused IAM market, is steeped in many of the drivers associated with business efficiency. Employees are often seen as the *inside-out* catalysts for business growth. By reducing the costs associated with employee management, an organisation can become more efficient, driving scarce resources into the areas within the business that drive customer acquisition, servicing and stickiness–which ultimately drives revenue.

So when does IAM become CIAM?

Comparison of CIAM to IAM

Outside-in -v- Inside-out

CIAM is subtly different to IAM. Whilst the capabilities are somewhat similar and may overlap, CIAM capabilities are primarily focused on an *outside-in* perspective. Outside-in, as the origin of change is external to the core business–primarily the consumers of the good or service that is being created.

Figure 1.6: Outside-in versus Inside-out business identity forces:

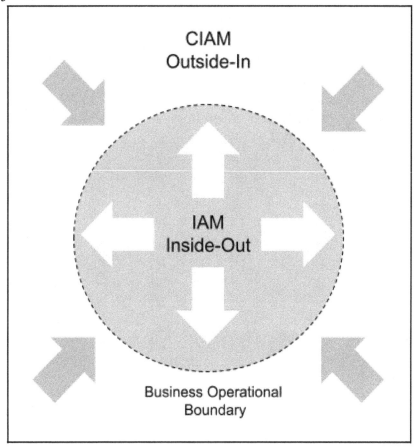

CIAM
Outside-In

IAM
Inside-Out

Business Operational
Boundary

Both CIAM and IAM are clearly focused on an identity. Both can be bound to the main identity functions of *who, what, where, why* and *when*. The capabilities and more importantly the drivers for usage, are subtly different however—but let us first take a look at a basic "W⁵" matrix, mapping the different identity types to the corresponding functions.

Figure 1.7 Who, What, Where, Why & When Matrix:

Function	CIAM description	IAM description
Who	Consumer, citizen or customer	Employee or contractor
What	Their own data, purchased product or service	Application or service for job completion
Where	Any internet location	Office location, some home access
Why	Personal experience	Job task completion
When	24 x 7 x 365 (limited down time)	8am–6pm, ~250 days per year (large maintenance windows)

The immediate obvious difference in *figure 1.7* is the user community now exists outside of the relatively controlled ecosystem of an organization. That in turn brings subtle differences in requirements and capabilities.

Figure 1.8 Difference in identity characteristics between CIAM and IAM:

Feature	CIAM	IAM
Volume of users	In the millions	In the thousands or tens of thousands
System throughput	000's transactions per sec	00's transactions per sec
No. of apps accessed	< 10	> 50
Assurance	Starts from anonymous	Starts from trusted HR system or contractor management system
Data ownership	End user	Organisation

Figure 1.8 describes some of the high level differences, specifically with regards to identity characteristics. Whilst an employee IAM system is focused, controlled and complex, consumer IAM is somewhat broader in scale, but shallower with regards to depth of application integration and workflow.

Functional & Non-functional

CIAM is also focused on delivering slightly different capabilities that map to different outcomes. Whilst employee IAM is driven primarily by operational efficiency, compliance and business facilitation, CIAM is built upon a user first mindset, that will ultimately help drive revenue for the organisation.

We will discuss CIAM drivers in more detail in the following section, but it is worth considering that the outcomes of a CIAM system will drive not only the demand for capabilities, but also the priority in how those capabilities are deployed and used.

But what is the CIAM system being used for? Typically it is to create a vehicle that allows an organisation to engage a specific user community, with the aim of delivering a product or service. Primarily this is a product or service with commercial gain, but CIAM is also being heavily used in non-profit sectors too, such as citizen engagement platforms run by central and local government.

In either ecosystem, the outcome of the CIAM system is based upon *user centricity*. That is, personalisation is an anchor feature, with the user driving how products are designed. An employee IAM system however, is likely to be more focused upon delivering *system centric* outcomes, with automation being a primary feature.

Figure 1.9 Example functional and non-functional capabilities overlap between CIAM and IAM:

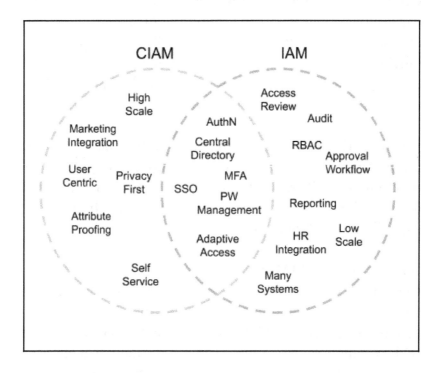

The functional and non-functional similarities (and differences) are often simple to quantify when using a technical lense. It is quite common to think in terms of features, products and solutions when faced with a technical problem. The nuances in the difference between CIAM and IAM can often be overlooked when using just a technical focus.

Whilst technology implementation may share API patterns and potentially different instances of the same solution, the operational ownership, budget control, service design and key success metrics will vary widely between the two ecosystems.

Business & Budget Owners

The business and budget owners of a CIAM system will invariably be different, mainly due to the outcomes a CIAM system is looking to achieve. As CIAM is *user centric* in nature, looking from *outside-in* perspective, a primary objective is often associated with user engagement. Key success metrics are likely to be associated with sign up rates and user acquisition, the number of successful authentications being made or the ratio between automated and real user interactions.

The business owners are likely to reside in outside-in focused teams–teams working within digital enablement, application design and marketing–where the natural focus is on attracting users to a service or product and removing any barriers to entry, purchase or understanding.

Whilst overlapping capabilities such as authentication, signup and password reset will often exist when compared against an employee IAM system, the design of those capabilities will be fundamentally different, simply as the business stakeholders will see those capabilities as secondary to a focus upon user happiness.

As the operational design will often sit within a different part of the organisation to that of employee IAM, so too, will the budget responsibility. The costs of CIAM technology should be closely aligned to the value derived from such a system—whether via a purchased commercial of the shelf (COTS) product, or via a home grown solution.

As the return on investment (RoI) will be seen from an outside-in perspective, with an ultimate goal of revenue generation or an increase in service utilisation, the available budget for a CIAM system may well be higher than that of an IAM system.

Why might that be? As described in *figure 1.5*, the drivers for employee IAM, are often associated with efficiency, systemization and cost reduction. The value of the employee IAM system is ultimately driven by the long term savings that are materialised.

Figure 1.10 Example operational and investment costs of employee IAM:

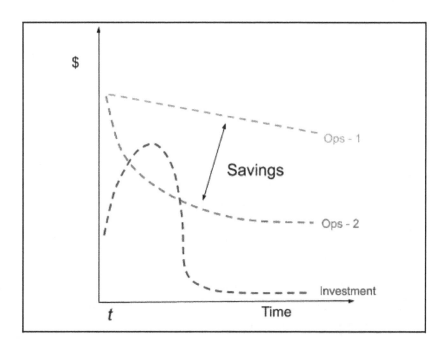

Figure 1.10 describes an example cost structure of an employee IAM system, looking at the everyday operational costs associated with fulfilling employee IAM related capabilities.

At an early Time-t, the everyday operational costs without any IAM investment (Ops–1) are high–perhaps due to a lack of process, manual execution or industrialization–and achieve only a small linear decrease over time, via improved personnel experience and written process.

If an organisation engages in an employee IAM investment project–as shown by the Investment line–initial costs will be high. Software licenses, project initiation, external consultancy and so on, will scc an immediate hump, with little impact on operational efficiency. However, clearly over time, an expected RoI (as shown between Ops–1 and Ops–2) should occur, measurable at the most basic level, as the reduction in everyday operational expense.

This assumes that the primary focus of the employee IAM is for business facilitation.

With respect to CIAM project cost discussion, a slightly different set of assumptions are made. As CIAM is focused on the *outside-in*, revenue and service usage are the primary success metrics being used. The investment analysis therefore, is a comparison against what future revenues could be generated, versus the cost savings achieved. Is a dollar created worth more than a dollar saved? Most CEO's would say "hell yeah".

Figure 1.11 Example operational and investment consumption of consumer IAM:

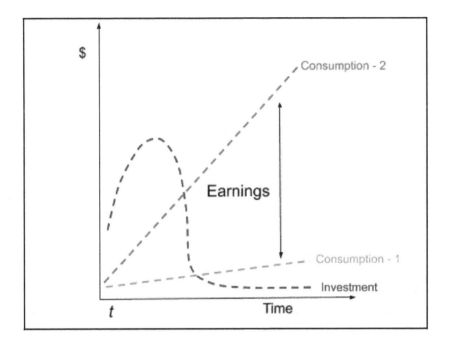

In *figure 1.11*, Consumption–1, is the usage (and potential revenue) of an outward facing service or product, without the support of a dedicated CIAM project investment. A basic linear increase may be observed, purely via organic growth. If CIAM investment occurred via the Investment line, again with *figure 1.10*, an initial hump is observed, followed up by a long tail of support and maintenance costs. The RoI in this example though, is focused upon the earnings, as shown as the difference between Consumption–1 and Consumption–2. Consumption–2 is driven by higher adoption, influenced by better user experience, scalability and security.

CIAM—Why Now?

Nearly all organisations operate under the most basic strategic initiative of optimizing efficiency and reducing cost. Many others, depending on age, size and sector will also simultaneously be focused on generating revenue. Both can be accomplished with sound investment in IAM technology—so why has CIAM developed into a multi-billion dollar industry in recent years?

Drivers

The Digital Journey

Of the 1.7 billion websites online in mid 2020[10], coupled with the ~4.5 billion internet users[11], a fair assumption can be made, that digitization has spread to nearly every interaction in modern society. Finance, banking, insurance, retail, dating, government, education and media all have a long list of exemplar services that are now either originating online or are performed entirely online.

Outbound Marketing

Digitization is certainly a journey, however. The creeping edge of digitization had its origins in a more outbound role for organisations looking to raise their brand, message and

10 https://www.internetlivestats.com/watch/websites/
11 https://www.internetlivestats.com/watch/internet-users/

audience reach. The digital aspect originated from *within* the organisation, and flowed from an inside-out perspective, through outbound marketing, brand awareness and audience specific content and copy. The main aim was to reach customers via a digital channel, but not necessarily complete the transaction online.

Self Service

Beyond the initial digital marketing narrative—which was often aimed at anonymous prospects—came a range of secondary digital engagement trends. Concepts such as loyalty schemes are not new, but being able to view and manage reward points online started to become a competitive differentiator. Other secondary engagement services included things like self service—being able to change a mailing address online for example—started the mechanics and end user education, that completing entire transactions online, was not far away.

Multi-channel

The process of being able to at least start a transaction online requires multiple subtle deployment options for a service provider. Many retailers and retail bankers for example, operate both a physical and digital presence simultaneously. Switching entirely from "bricks to bytes", would be a huge business risk and generate a level of operational complexity that could not be sustained.

Multi-channel operations allowed for the simultaneous delivery of existing modes of interaction, with newer and more diverse online interactions–often aimed at new audiences as part of a business development initiative.

The subtlety this brought, is that both channels did not need to resemble one another. A customer familiar with a physical branch experience within banking, was set the expectation that an online experience would be suitably different and that an active choice would need to be made to use that channel–along with the potential limitations and differences that may have brought.

Omnichannel

Multi-channel is often the selected state for many organisations and they may operate in this manner for a number of years, due to industry, customer and competitive demands. An omnichannel experience moves towards a more integrated experience that offers a "cross-channel content strategy that organizations use to improve their user experience and drive better relationships with their audience across points of contact"[12]. Initiating a process on a mobile device and ending up within a physical store, where an assistant has a full history of what was completed online, is a simple example of a seamless and joined up omnichannel experience.

An omnichannel experience is heavily reliant on being able to know your customer (KYC), capture their *wants* and *needs*, analyse their past and current behaviour (in order to

[12] https://en.wikipedia.org/wiki/Omnichannel

predict future trends) and ultimately deliver a personalised and empathetic experience.

So within the digital journey maturity model, why is omnichannel deemed most attractive?

By being able to deliver a more value focused interaction and personalised experience, the service provider is able to engage both existing and prospective consumers. Through increased engagement comes increased stickiness, where a consumer is less likely to move to a competitor and more likely to refer and recommend.

As omnichannel is so coupled with delivering entire services digitally, a higher degree of agility becomes the new operating normal.

Competitive Agility

Increased use of digitization within the service delivery model, places a greater need on being agile, as well as agile itself being a driver for digital experiences. Whilst being operationally agile is not necessarily the same as software development agility[13], both share a common origin–that of tackling *complex* and *unknown* problems.

Agility can be seen as a response to a type information failure[14], where a set of data points have unknown characteristics to one side of a transaction. In the case of digital service delivery, the unknown aspect often comes from speculative investment with regards to new services,

13https://en.wikipedia.org/wiki/Agile_software_development
14https://www.economicshelp.org/blog/glossary/information-failure/

offerings, applications and products.

If we launch something new, will the customer like it? If they don't, can we change the product so they do like it? How do we capture their feedback? If the competition launches something new, can we respond in a timely fashion?

Organisations in every sector face competitive pressure. Established industries are facing threats from smaller more agile innovators, who, without existing revenue models and customer inertia, can "unbundle and decouple"[15] larger platform based products and solutions, into smaller more value focused blocks.

A smaller, more digitally minded innovator, is often able to split the value and non-value generating blocks from a customer transaction. Not only can they protect existing revenue streams through digital conversion, they can also look to make more adventurous and potentially risky service launches, in the knowledge they can be easily reverted or altered based on usage and demand.

---

15 https://www.hbs.edu/faculty/Publication%20Files/15-031_accfb920-4667-4ccb-b2e1-453984a1879f.pdf

Figure 1.12 Example decoupling of shopping experience:

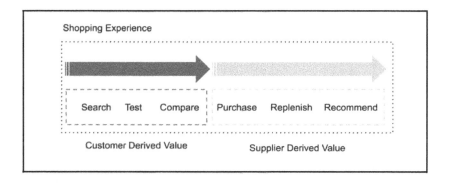

In *figure 1.12* the traditional physical shopping experience can be broken down into the value derived to both the *consumer* of the product and the *supplier*. The typical search, test and compare stages provide insight and knowledge to the consumer, who would typically then follow those steps with transaction completion in store, perhaps coerced via the store consultant who has provided valuable product knowledge.

In a digitally decoupled landscape, perhaps the test and compare process is still completed in store, but with the purchase and replenish steps being completed via an online service, that offers a cheaper price. The supplier-derived value is captured without the costs of providing a store front for browsing, testing and comparison.

Digital agility in this case, helps to either create the supplier-derived value components natively or can stop a decoupled competitor developing them and capturing market share.

Any components developed on the supplier derived value block, will be heavily dependent on a CIAM infrastructure to build KYC, purchasing and referral systems.

Benefits of CIAM

The benefits of a CIAM investment initiative are really embedded alongside the benefits associated with delivering those digital omnichannel experiences. Let us break down the analysis from two lenses—one focused on the benefits to the service provider and another looking from an end user perspective

For The Provider

Service Protection & Innovation

> By engaging in a digital delivery model where a foundation for long term customer derived value can be created, service adoption or revenue can be protected and increased. By focusing on how to split both the customer and supplier *value* chain components within a service, allows competitive threats to be tackled, through increased business agility.

Response to Change

> Change is facing organisations from many angles though, not just competitive disruption. Technology

in general—in the form cloud services, mobile first, big data and artificial intelligence—are just a few of the potentially existential concerns executive teams need to address, if they are to survive and thrive.

By embracing a digital first delivery model, where CIAM is the foundation for user interaction, a more flexible and cost effective way to adapt to external challenges can be leveraged, with a "fail fast, fail hard" approach to overcoming external change.

Unknown Threat Protection

A further extension to the ability to respond to change, is the increasing number of "unknown unknowns". Unknown unknowns are "risks that come from situations that are so unexpected that they would not be considered."[16] The focus here tends to be on existential rare events, such as the 2020 outbreak of Covid-19, but can often come in the form of political and social change, like unexpected industry regulation or viral driven cultural events. By being in control of a digital CIAM experience, organisations can spend more time preparing and less time predicting threats.

Digitization and CIAM essentially allows an organisation to develop into a more fluid and market response driven

16https://en.wikipedia.org/wiki/There_are_known_knowns

organisation, that is capable of responding (and not reacting) to external forces, such as changing demand, competitive pressures or catastrophic events.

For The End User

Age of the Consumer

> Digitization has seen the term the "age of the consumer"[17] enter the business landscape–where customer happiness is the foundation of successful business execution. If the service provider switched focus from a customer "sale", to post-sale happiness, the consumer is more likely to return, creating a sticky relationship and referring the provider to friends, family and colleagues. The role of the CEO effectively changes from the business operator to the end user–with all the decision making, control and choice switching too.

Personalisation

> On the back of delivering customer happiness and post-sales success, is personalisation. The psychological aspects of feeling special, using a service that knows your preferences, nuanced choices and "digital personality" has a significant impact on retention and churn reduction. People never forget how something made them feel and

17 https://www.marketing-interactive.com/what-does-the-age-of-the-consumer-really-mean

personalisation is a key benefit of a focused service. However, for services to deliver personalisation, they must first gather and analyse vast amounts of consumer information, pertaining to behaviour and choice. We will discuss the privacy and consent aspects of this in later chapters.

Everything on Demand

The rise of media services (radio, films, TV, music) which are delivered in a personalised and on-demand fashion is significant and a good exemplar of the "on demand" paradigm. The music industry has been selling access to music for over 100 years since the age of the gramophone and it is fascinating to observe continued iteration in how organisations such as Spotify, Apple Music, Tidal and others are innovating. Coming back to *figure 1.12*, where we split consumer value and provider value, in the case of radio for example, the consumer value was the song, the service provider value was the advertising opportunity in between tracks. By switching to a decoupled model of delivery, the consumer value is split out, allowing not only a personalised ad free experience, but also allows the listener access to more songs, at a time of their choosing.

CIAM essentially brings control and choice to the end user. They are essentially empowered to be "one click" away from a competitive service or product and have access to more product, service and market information than ever before, in order to allow better decision making.

Challenges

So, if the benefits of CIAM can be observed on both sides of the economic transaction, what are the challenges to success and adoption for an organisation?

Legacy technology

> The first obvious one is technology delivery. We will discuss some of the detailed requirements and architectures of a CIAM solution in later chapters, but certain technology requirements need to be met in order to deliver agile, scalable and secure identity services. This could include dedicated commercial off the shelf solutions or home grown integrations, but they will often require new deployments and design. Existing IAM solutions applied to the employee outside-in ecosystem, tend not to fare well in a CIAM setting and often fail to deliver the necessary use cases.

Organisational Structure

> As CIAM is often focused on the *inside-out* user interactions, there are new key performance indicators (KPI's), metrics and success outcomes associated with it. But many organisations struggle to identify where in the organisation CIAM should operate and who should own the metrics and

outcomes. Many organisations start with operating CIAM from a digital development area, often focused on delivering mobile, single page and modern web applications. Is this the optimum area for ownership?

Skills

Not only does CIAM generate new technical and organisational demands, the skills within the supporting organisation also need innovating to take on the delivery of new services. Every step of the service delivery journey would need new skills being learnt and applied. Business analysis, product ownership, software development, application integration and generic run/operate capabilities, will all need a new CIAM focused lens being applied.

In general, organisations are moving from solving known problems (focused on workforce enablement and business facilitation) to unknown problems (focused on external service delivery) and all the facets that entails. CIAM requires a top down cultural change within an organisation as they move towards delivering digital customer success.

Real World Examples

In order to highlight some of the core capabilities and use cases of a CIAM system, let us walk through some real world examples of CIAM use, from organisational concepts we should all be relatively familiar with.

ACME Bank

Let us start with something that is a key pillar of a developed economy: a retail bank.

ACME Bank provides banking services primarily to consumers and citizens within one country. It has a long history, having been founded in the United Kingdom in 1899. It has undergone numerous transformations in it's ~120 year history, having performed acquisitions and mergers with numerous competitors.

Let us break down the main *objectives*, *strategies* and *tactics*[18] of the bank for the next 3 years and how they could leverage a CIAM foundation to achieve success.

---

[18]https://www.linkedin.com/pulse/why-strategic-thinking-so-important-simon-moffatt-cissp/

Figure 1.13 Acme Bank Objectives, Strategies, Tactics map:

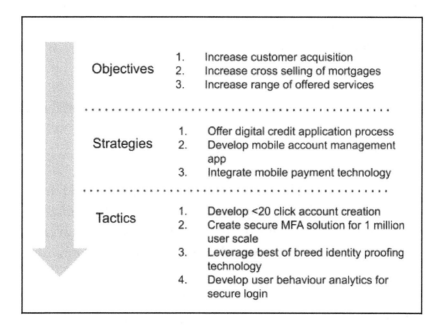

Figure 1.13 provides a range of opportunities that will rely heavily on being able to provide registration, account proofing and secure login services for a range of new digital offerings. The primary delivery vehicle will be a mobile application that will communicate to a cloud service over modern and responsive APIs. The application will deliver a range of services previously available via physical interactions at bank branches or automatic teller machines (ATM's), such as money transfer, balance checking, payee creation, standing order management and statement ordering.

In addition, future use cases will include the mobile application being used to make payments at point of sale terminals via NFC (near field communication) available via modern smartphones. The banking application will allow payments after a successful biometric fingerprint login and after performing background transaction and usage behaviour analytics.

The bank aims to attract 50,000 new customers within 2 years of launch and aims to service more than 1 million active users per month.

Some immediate challenges in design would include *scale*, *security* and *agility*. Being able to roll out frequent changes to the mobile application (new identity proofing services, secure authentication) would also be a prerequisite. It is likely that rapid spikes in both registration and login activity, would be experienced during marketing promotions and during large scale spending events such as summer vacations and public holidays.

Government of the United Mountains

Not all CIAM solutions are focused on revenue and new competitive pressures. Central and regional government services are migrating to a digital first delivery model, in order to reduce cost, increase reach and engagement and expand the range of services being offered.

Many governments face continual downward pressure on funding, whilst simultaneously face consistent pressures with regards to increasing populations, a broader array of services to manage as well as being compared to private enterprise when it comes to service orchestration and management performance.

Figure 1.14 Government of the United Mountains Objectives, Strategies and Tactics map:

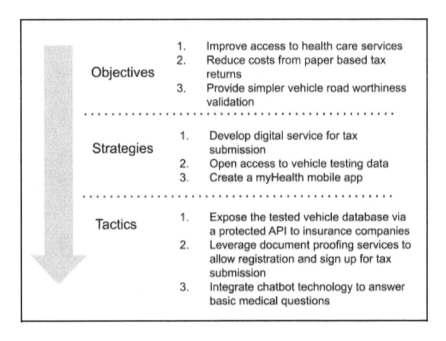

Figure 1.14 shows a typical 3 year plan for a large central government department delivering services for a developed economy with over 25 million citizens.

The technical aspects are often only one angle to service delivery within government. The RoI and key success metrics clearly can't be measured in revenue and profit and instead need to focus on citizen needs, service usage, adoption and accessibility, whilst staying within a shrinking year-on-year budget.

Government designed digital CIAM services often need to focus upon long term stability, planning for unknown changes in usage and behaviour and being able to integrate newer tools and practices without redesigning core infrastructure.

From a technical perspective, *figure 1.14* highlights a clear need for two way trust–identity proofing and validation from a service provider perspective with regards to preventing tax fraud–and from an end user perspective, privacy and security associated with the sharing of basic medical needs over a mobile application. These capabilities are likely to change rapidly due to advances in innovation, and would need to be modular enough for rapid iteration.

The concept of exposing the vehicle testing database semi-publically also generates a range of challenges–operationally and technically. Technically, authentication, authorization and rate limiting would be needed to protect an API (application programming interface), as well as the ability to identify, enroll and manage access to trusted insurance organisations who would use the data as part of car premium generation.

Operationally, that service would need to manage relationships, service level agreements and contracting with the entities the data was made available to. If that process was part of a commercial relationship, digital product owners would also be needed to work with customer demand and functionality requirements.

As with all government related services, usage metrics tend to be higher than most CIAM solutions and certainly considerably higher than employee focused IAM. Central directories for user profiles, generally need to scale to more than 20 million records and active daily use to be around 10% of that. Spikes in usage also need to be considered, especially with regards to services like taxation where periodic events like returns due dates cause large changes in demand.

Summary

This chapter was focused on the rudimentary concepts of consumer identity and access management, the primary differences with the more mature employee focused identity and access industry and the trends and challenges facing both private and public sector entities on their CIAM journey.

The preceding chapters will focus upon the requirements of a successful solution as well a detailed analysis of designing and selecting trusted vendors and providers.

CHAPTER 2

Existing Approaches to CIAM

This chapter will focus upon some of the existing approaches to addressing CIAM related solution design, and also take a brief look at emerging and future trends. Whilst CIAM has gained popularity in recent years, with a dedicated set of suppliers and analyst commentary, the capabilities were often being deployed in many emerging states prior to 2013, either in the form of home grown solutions, or bespoke supplier deployed integrations. Since then, a relative level of maturity has emerged, supplying different commercial off the shelf (COTS) products and integrated solutions.

We will take a journey that starts from home grown solutions and ends up analysing the current market for dedicated CIAM solutions, commenting on some of the pro's and con's of each deployment option and why they have emerged.

Home Grown Solutions

Let us start with the scenario of a home grown solution. Organisations in all sectors and all sizes, invest in home grown solutions for a range of capabilities, not just related to CIAM. Data management, mobile applications and business workflow amongst others, have all been attacked by in house development teams.

Why Do Home Grown CIAM Solutions Exist?

So why do home grown CIAM solutions exist? I think that question needs to be broken down into two distinct eras. Firstly, like most solutions, there would be an era before commercialisation existed–where the market for procuring an off the shelf product, that solved the majority of the required use cases may not have existed. Clearly a second area of analysis is why decide to develop in house, if a commercial solution *did exist* and could be procured?

Small Scoped Project

Let us start with the case of a small scoped CIAM project. The project origins are likely to reside within a single home grown developed application, that is internet facing. Perhaps a mobile application, or web site that is to be used by end users who are not under the control of the organisation. The users of this application could be buyers of a product or consumers or commentators on supplied content. The application is siloed and has no further interactions to other applications with limited end user analytics requirements. In this scenario, a tactical approach to building registration, login, user storage and password reset capabilities could reside within the existing application development team. The cost of even researching and analysing a viable external alternative may well be higher than developing the tactical capabilities and as such commercial solutions are not even considered, if indeed they existed.

Lack of Suitable Alternatives

As technical capabilities grow, perhaps with increases in user scale, the number of applications being integrated or new security and compliance drivers, analysis of external offerings starts to become a credible research activity. However, a suitable market alternative may not exist. Market maturity may not have reached a position where a repeatable set of use cases, deployment patterns and licensing options attract suppliers to the market. The early requirements for CIAM, were likely to be focused on "glue-ware"–where the integration of existing systems was a key priority. The integration of the newly built external facing application to internal marketing and CRM (customer relationship management) systems is likely to be highly customized, achieved by connectors, single use applications and scripting in order to fulfill data pipeline requirements. A lack of market maturity and the ability for buyers to compare home grown requirements to supplier offerings likely lead to further inhouse development.

Lack of Organisational Maturity

When it comes to the procurement of commercial software, a bidirectional level of maturity is required. For the buyer to initiate a market analysis process, assumes a deep understanding of their requirements, use cases and operational demands. Does the organisation know the short, medium and long term roadmap of functional and non-functional requirements their CIAM system should fulfil? Has a budget been allocated? Does a dedicated team exist that can consume, operationalise and integrate with a third party provided system? Another key requirement of procuring a CIAM system, would be success measurement. How would a successful deployment be measured? What metrics and key performance indicators (KPI's) would be used to hold the vendor to account to help calculate total cost of ownership (TCO) and returns on investment (ROI)? If these are lacking, the ability to engage a supplier would be hampered.

Customization Trumps COTS

As the supplier and organisational demands mature, a level of alignment may not always be forthcoming however. As suppliers develop a set of foundational use cases and repeatable deployment patterns, organisational integration requirements are also becoming more complex. Not only are technical requirements evolving–perhaps focused on password-less authentication, consent management or compliance to emerging requirements such as the GDPR[19] (General Data Protection Regulation)–so too are operational needs. Existing home grown

19 https://eur-lex.europa.eu/eli/reg/2016/679/oj

solutions need migrating, updating and integrating. Customizations focused on end user experience, usability and sector specific omnichannel experiences, ramp up the post procurement integration effort. Often the short and long term cost of in-house effort, can still be less than the total cost of ownership of a COTS system, if a long tale of existing development and expertise exists.

(Cost of COTS Initial Procurement + Support) < ((Cost of In-house People + Infrastructure) + (Opportunity Cost)) -> *Drives external supplier demand*

(Cost of COTS Initial Procurement + Support + *Customization*) > ((Cost of In-house People + Infrastructure) + (Opportunity Cost)) -> *Drives in house development*

The opportunity cost[20] from investing in staff and infrastructure to build a home grown CIAM solution, will often remove the ability for that cost to be spent on other areas of the organisation. That cost could be significant and is often difficult to quantify.

There is often the conception however, that whilst a home grown solution provides immediacy and room for customization, it could actually lead to a lack of future proofing and extensibility coupled with longer term integration and support costs.

20https://en.wikipedia.org/wiki/Opportunity_cost

Certainly for complex components such as cryptography, there is a default industry axiom of "don't roll your own"[21], but cryptography is likely a specialist example however, where the concept of the Kerckhoff Principle[22] is often applied. This principle basically states that the entire system should have a significant level of transparency associated with it. Transparency is seen to help remove error, improve efficiency and structure by the simple virtue of peer review and impartial analysis.

The transparency aspect could be achieved by building upon agreed and ratified industry standards or via the open sourcing of libraries. So if you are applying those concepts to a home grown CIAM system, does that overcome any negative long term cost?

The Implications of Home Grown

Let us take a look at some of the implications of developing a home grown CIAM solution.

Revenue Generator

> If we extend the discussion around the opportunity cost of home grown CIAM development, we can end up with a question that ultimately revolves around "can the tooling that was built be sold?".

---

21 https://www.vice.com/en_us/article/wnx8nq/why-you-dont-roll-your-own-crypto
22 https://en.wikipedia.org/wiki/Kerckhoffs%27s_principle

This is really trying to identify if the costs that were sunk into inhouse development, can be recouped in some way, in order to increase corporate profitability. The answer is likely no–unless of course you happen to be a CIAM vendor–but is that the end of the story? Can the opportunity cost be measured in other ways? Can the intellectual property generated by home grown development be captured elsewhere? One way of looking at a home grown system, could be classifying the CIAM system as an asset–and in turn it could potentially be used for depreciation calculations on accountancy returns. If the asset can't be quantified immediately, does the investment in an inhouse system provide enough long term savings to make it worthwhile? Does the home grown system allow the applications it powers to generate enough revenue to be worthwhile?

Ability to Extend and Expand

As with any system, the functionality and capabilities required by a CIAM solution, are likely to change over time. As we discussed in chapter 1, CIAM is often deeply embedded with digitization and a transformative approach to customer acquisition. But customer needs change rapidly. Can the home grown solution respond to competitive pressures, changes in user growth, external compliance requirements or new technical mega trends? Some examples of recent technical changes could include the movement to being cloud, mobile and API ready. Emerging security threats too, such as the use of AI/ML (artificial intelligence/ machine learning) on the adversary side can expose a lack of adaptability.

Data Silos

If the origin of many home grown CIAM solutions is often within a single application or target audience, a lack of extensibility and further integration may exist. This can lead to two-way data siloing. Firstly the inbound user experience is often tied to a single application journey—no single sign on, cross brand interaction or omnichannel experience is possible and the end user experience becomes degraded and repetitive, if individual usernames, passwords and registration is needed per application. From an organisational perspective, multiple identity repositories may exist, to support deployments built for individual applications. A "John Smith" in application 1, may well be "John Smith101" in application 2, rendering analytics and data correlation complexities. Not only does the organisation have to service redundant data sources, the end user encounters a disjointed set of interactions that lack personalisation.

Predictability in Costs

We have mentioned costs several times in this

chapter and they are a considerable part of the home grown narrative. A major component of cost analysis when it comes to a CIAM solution is trying to dampen *cost surprise*–by focusing on the preparation and not prediction of future events. The initial cost of setting up basic user registration, login and identity storage capabilities, may well be very low, when compared to the entire cost of launching a new mobile application for example. However, are the longer term running, operational and support costs known? What happens if the user population rapidly spikes and requires a 10x increase in profile storage space? What happens if the user activity rates increase due to a marketing event resulting in a 5x increase in logins per second? Are your personnel costs that fulfill CIAM operations known and can you hire at a timely and cost effective rate? Analysis of potential hidden costs should be performed up front.

As we come to the end of the analysis on home grown solutions, let us try and summarise our thinking, by creating a checklist, to help analyze the rationale of developing a home grown CIAM solution or analysing COTS offerings.

Home Grown CIAM Checklist

1. Does the organisation have existing expertise in designing identity and access management capabilities?
2. Does the organisation have an existing operational

team to support ongoing CIAM functions?

3. Does the organisation have an allocated budget for CIAM based solutions?
4. Does the organisation have success metrics for systems that will use CIAM capabilities?
5. Does the organisation have to adhere to external security or compliance requirements?
6. Has the organisation had experience in building external facing applications?
7. Is the profile of the application end users known? (Eg. volume, usage, location, growth pattern, habits)
8. Are the current and future requirements for the CIAM system known? (Eg. integrations, security, usability, access control)

The above checklist can act as a hypothetical exercise in order to understand existing requirements and drivers for considering home grown CIAM investment.

Figure 2.1 CIAM Build versus Buy High Level Comparison

Build		Buy	
Pro	Con	Pro	Con
Ability to customize	Lack of best practice	Specialised product	High initial cost
Quicker start	Long term support costs	Evolving feature set	Lack of customization

Build up of intellectual property	Personnel dependent	Secure and scalable	Vendor lockin
Initial cost saving	Future capability	Outsource risk	Difficult to migrate

Employee Identity Systems

Let us move onto another approach to CIAM, which is often associated with the teams, budgets and suppliers of existing employee IAM. In chapter 1 we discussed some of the key operational, functional and nonfunctional differences between CIAM and IAM. By association it should be clear that employee IAM is not always a suitable delivery vehicle for large scale complex CIAM projects. Let us discuss, however, why they are often considered and used in such projects.

Organisational Maturity

As we discussed when analysing some of the drivers of home grown solutions, organisational maturity has again a large role to play in why employee IAM is often utilised to service CIAM use cases. As CIAM requirements mature, and outgrow the ability of a single application development team, application and business owners will often look internally to find a location where CIAM operational ownership could reside. Ownership would entail the deployment, business as usual (BAU) support and associated costs of fulfilling the CIAM service catalogue, as well creating a pillar of accountability with regards to success metrics. As employee IAM is more mature, has clear roles and responsibilities and budgetary control, employee IAM teams are often "saddled" with delivering the early incarnations of CIAM, simply as no other capable organisational unit exists. This is a distant cousin of Conway's Law[23], where a system design often resembles the existing organisational communication channels. As employee IAM has strong lines of communication from the executive team right down to implementation, those channels are being duplexed with CIAM demands.

Sunk Costs

One of the key issues with CIAM design and deployment, is often knowing the future state. This would include future user numbers, throughput, application activity, associated revenue projections and so on. As with developing a home grown solution, the long term success criteria of an application using CIAM capabilities may not be known. As such, they may have a low appetite to invest large amounts in either a bespoke system or a simple COTS product. That CIAM cost may not be budgeted and if budgeted, difficult to justify. As a result, business and application owners, may look

23 https://en.wikipedia.org/wiki/Conway%27s_law

for existing sunk costs[24] within the organisation that could absorb the required investment. Those sunk costs may well be associated with the existing employee IAM systems, especially if their utilisation is perceived to be low or hard to measure. As most large (10,000 employee) organisations will have dedicated employee IAM tools, teams and infrastructure, CIAM may be cross mapped in this way.

Specialist Expertise

Whilst employee IAM and CIAM are fundamentally different, there are of course some overlaps with regards to capabilities and required expertise. IAM of any flavour requires a specialist set of skills, that neither application developers nor pure play information security practitioners will necessarily possess. Fundamental concepts such as authentication, authorization, identity data governance and identity data storage, will apply to both ecosystems and those skills are likely to reside within the employee IAM deployment teams. Whilst we discussed the fundamental differences in chapter 1–namely the *system* (employee IAM) versus *user* (CIAM) centricity–employee IAM engineers could possibly be the most likely within a large organisation to transition into CIAM related projects.

24 https://www.investopedia.com/terms/s/sunkcost.asp

Figure 2.2 Employee IAM High Level Comparison

Employee IAM	
Pro	Con
Existing operational teams in place	Focused on systems not users
Foundational skills in identity	Differing security and scale capabilities
Mature systems	Focused on efficiency not revenue generation
Procurement processes in place	Lack of marketing, CRM & analytics experience

Overall, the scale, security and operational integration lines, for departments such as marketing, customer analytics and product development, are often lacking when it comes to standard employee IAM. Budgetary control is different as are the key success metrics, resulting in fundamental mismatches in technical capabilities as well as operational control between employee lead and consumer lead IAM.

Specialist Suppliers

Let us switch gears and start to analyse some of the more specialist CIAM providers. CIAM providers can be broken down into several different areas–based on delivery models, capabilities and origins. By the end of this section, we will aim to provide a basic understanding of the CIAM market, before analysing some of the dedicated suppliers.

Core CIAM Capabilities

We can expand on the capabilities introduced in *chapter 1,* by digging a little deeper into what a CIAM should attempt to deliver. Most CIAM solutions will typically be internet facing, accessible via a range of different device types and cater to a varied and distributed user base. The organisation delivering the service or product, will likely require deep knowledge and analytics of the user activity, in order to deliver a personalised experience and identify revenue opportunities and service iteration. All of which will drive a need for strong privacy and consent functionality, in addition to the standard security principles.

So, let us break down some key CIAM capabilities into both the functional and non-functional aspects before we start to analyse the origins of some of the CIAM providers.

Functional

"Lite" & Progressive Registration

> Getting users to register for a service can be difficult enough, without placing additional barriers in the form of time consuming registration flows.

Registration journeys should capture information using a "just-in-time" paradigm, removing initial large data capture events (often via tedious and repetitive forms), with lean processing. Social identity providers (IDPs) as initial attribute and profile creation sources, can help streamline the signup process too, commonly known as bring your own identity (BYOI). Subsequent touch points with the end user will also generate opportunities to verify existing data or capture new data, based on transaction or time. The incremental capturing of data during subsequent login events, is often known as "smart" or "progressive" profiling—only capturing data when you need it. All profile data, regardless of how it was captured, will be continually "proofed" by document, pictorial or in-person equivalent assurance systems.

Profile & Data Management

Once a user is registered and using a service, the "age of the consumer" drives a "data on demand" mentality. The user will require *visibility* and *control* into the data the service provider has collected on them. This will range from basic personal identifiable information (PII)—with clear and accessible self service for changeability and revocation—through to understanding and changing first and third party access to system activity data too. The information used for registration and login events, will often be augmented with secondary and tertiary data, covering addresses, devices, transactions, usage, analytics and more.

Consent Lifecycle

Regulations such as the GDPR and California Consumer Protection Act[25] (CCPA) are upholding data control of the end user. Any CIAM solution needs to provide consent *capture*, *storage* and *revocation* capabilities to comply with correct personal data handling. All first and third party uses of individual user data will need to be explicitly described to the end user, whilst providing the ability to allow, deny and revoke any granted permissions. The more data the service provider captures and uses, the more complex the consent management capabilities required.

Privacy By Design

User data—including and especially with regard to service usage and activity—will likely be highly valuable to the service owner and the associated third party ecosystem. Even whilst operating under a mature consent management framework, a mature CIAM solution will also need the necessary privacy preservation functionality such as data tokenization or even more recent approaches to data privacy such as homomorphic encryption[26]. This

25 https://oag.ca.gov/privacy/ccpa
26 https://en.wikipedia.org/wiki/Homomorphic_encryption

requirement becomes more pressing as the federated collection of different data pipeline integrations grows.

Secure By Default

Modern security architectures leverage identity and access management at their foundation. Consumer facing systems will be exposed to automated, repetitive and effective data security attacks. CIAM data is valuable! The use of multi-factor authentication (often applied to a strong customer authentication SCA[27] scenario), contextual analysis and adaptive access will be "table-stakes" functionality when it comes to protecting user information and ensuring brand trust is not damaged via avoidable data breaches. Multi-factor authentication options are likely to be standards based—using the likes of fast identity online (FIDO) or WebAuthn—and also be modular and changeable to support continuing industry iteration. Authorization—applying runtime controls to enforce "who has access to what"—needs to be adaptive and flexible. Finally bot identification and account takeover (ATO) protection should be applied to all exposed services.

Omnichannel

Omnichannel is often an overused word, but when it

27 https://www.fca.org.uk/consumers/strong-customer-authentication

comes to the modern consumer experience, that is both personalised, yet friction free, the ability to deliver those interactions across a range of device types is essential. Those device types, may not also be the typical smartphone and tablet–increasingly internet of things (IoT) gadgets, connected cars, sensors and home automation systems also become part of the users expected touch points. These devices will need to be integrated into the user's journey, with the ability to pair, manage and revoke access and transferred data. Omnichannel by association, drives a need for server side components to be API-first in their design approach. By exposing services over APIs based on industry concepts such as REST/JSON, promotes integration across different device types, languages and libraries. These APIs of course need securing too.

Non Functional

Scale–Storage

User profile data storage should likely cater for a million users, even if active monthly users may be lower. The room for growth on an internet facing system will be considerably higher than that of an employee IAM system, where known patterns of user population change will be known. The ability to store multiple data attributes and links to orthogonal sources of data will also be key.

Scale–Usage

Another angle relating to scale, is system usage and throughput. Higher active user totals, will likely result in a requirement to support higher throughput–or transactions per second (TPS)–especially for services such as registration, password reset and authentication (login).

Distributed & Localised

CIAM is very rarely tied to a single geographical location or region. It tends to be distributed across multiple regions–often different counties–resulting in a need to deliver the same omnichannel experiences based on different languages, locales and culturally different usability experiences. Other basic capabilities with respect to distribution are likely–with the typical "London user" appearing in New York for a work trip, yet will expect the exact same set of services, at the same speed, friction free as if based at home.

Highly Available & Elastic

Whilst making a single application available 99.999% of the time is pretty typical, being able to support the same requirement for a complex CIAM middleware system may be somewhat more challenging. An orthogonal cousin of being highly available, is being *elastically* available. Elasticity refers to the ability to scale services up (and down) due to external changes in load–whilst still adhering to storage, usage and high availability requirements. An example being spikes in usage–perhaps registrations or login–driven by marketing campaigns or cultural events. Can a highly available system designed for 10,000 logins per second, cope if that number doubles or triples in a short period of time? If a system expands, is the converse true? Under light load, can resources be scaled back?

Integrated and Extendable

The identity data integrations for the CIAM system work in a bidirectional manner. Flows leaving the platform would include identity assertion and token data post login, along with profile data being synchronized to customer relationship management (CRM), marketing and analytics systems. Coming into the system would be profile data for registration, attribute proofing, risk analysis and contextual intelligence used during run time events. All of those interactions should leverage industry standards for interoperability and modularization and likely be API-first in design. We will cover the standards in detail in later chapters, but the likes of OAuth2, OpenID Connect, SCIM and LDAP would be common.

Market Breakdown

Before we can start to analyse the existing CIAM providers market, let us first expand on the origins of many of the suppliers. Like most market definitions, the capabilities aspect is only one part. The supplier driven qualities are equally important—and insightful—when it comes to analysing their offerings, propositions and industry roadmap.

Origins within IAM

As we discussed in *chapter 1* and earlier in the employee identity section, the market and feature set for IAM is large and mature and is often used—rightly or wrongly—for delivering CIAM related capabilities. Existing suppliers of IAM functionality would initially be focused on the overlapping set of capabilities between CIAM and IAM such as authentication, API protection using OAuth2/OIDC, identity data storage, SSO and adaptive and contextual authorization. Clearly there are numerous CIAM projects that will require considerably more functionality such as marketing and CRM integration, advanced self service, consent management and more. But for CIAM projects, often requiring user registration, user storage and login services, many existing IAM vendors started to provide SKU's (stock units/price options) for using the technology in external facing systems. Those services have now expanded to include CIAM specific capabilities such as being API first with mobile, consent and privacy capabilities.

Let us take a look (in alphabetic order) of some sample vendors in this genus.

Broadcom (formerly CA Technologies)

Broadcom was founded in 1991, is headquartered in San Francisco Bay Area and has made over 30 acquisitions[28], including CA Technologies and Symantec, where its identity management components now reside. The traditional focus was upon employee IAM, but in recent years has developed go to market strategies focused on harnessing its large back catalogue of software for consumer focused projects, with capabilities covering API Management, authentication, SSO, digital payments fraud, user storage directory and identity management[29].

ForgeRock

ForgeRock was founded in 2010 in Europe, but now has its headquarters in San Francisco, USA. ForgeRock was formed on the back of the Oracle acquisition of Sun Microsystems that was announced in 2009[30], where numerous pieces of Sun's open source middleware platform were later "end of life'd" in favour of Oracle's existing Fusion Middleware products. ForgeRock forked the open source openAM and openDS projects to lay the foundation of the ForgeRock Identity Platform[31]. Today the ForgeRock Identity Platform now provides identity management, access management,

28https://www.crunchbase.com/search/acquisitions/field/organizations/num_acquisitions/broadcom
29https://docs.broadcom.com/doc/harness-the-potential-of-consumer-identities
30https://www.oracle.com/corporate/pressrelease/oracle-buys-sun-042009.html
31https://www.forgerock.com/identity-and-access-management-platform

user storage and gateway protection functionality for both large scale employee IAM and CIAM focused projects, delivered via a cloud or on-premises delivery model.

IBM

IBM has a long history of delivering software and services since it was founded over 100 years ago. In recent years its IBM Security business unit delivers a range of CIAM related functionality[32] including Cloud Identity, Secret Server and its Identity Governance & Intelligence products. Cloud Identity provides a cloud delivered set of identity and access management capabilities, accessible using an API, that can be used to power CIAM based projects. The IBM Secret Server and Identity Governance areas focus on use cases related to privileged access management and identity certification, which may power related projects.

Micro Focus

Micro Focus is a UK based software company, founded in the 1970's–since which time it has acquired 14 companies[33]–one of which being Attachmate in 2014, who in turn had acquired the intellectual property of NetIQ in 2006. NetIQ had developed the NetIQ Access Manager and NetIQ Identity Manager products, initially focused on

[32]https://www.ibm.com/security/services/ciam-consumer-identity-and-access-management
[33]https://www.crunchbase.com/search/acquisitions/field/organizations/num_acquisitions/micro-focus

employee ecosystems. These products have now been positioned towards the CIAM space[34]. The NetIQ solution focuses on single sign on, federation, risk based authentication, multi factor authentication and mobile device integration.

Okta

Okta was founded in 2009 and went public in 2017. Its initial focus was on providing SSO services to cloud based resources for employees–all via a SaaS delivered platform. Since then it has added focus for business to business and secure CIAM related ecosystems[35]. Okta provides four main pillars of functionality, covering Social Authentication (allowing sign on and data capture from social networks), Universal Directory (for storing captured data and creating a centralised view of users), Signal Sign On (to allow a single session to be used across multiple systems) and Adaptive MFA (for applying varied security during login).

Ping Identity

Ping Identity is a US based (Denver) software vendor and cloud based services provider, founded in 2002 and became a publicly listed company in 2019. Their initial rise to prominence was centered around Ping Federate–capabilities focused on employee cross boundary access and single sign on.

---

34 https://www.microfocus.com/media/white-paper/
consumer_identity_and_access_management_turning_digital_business_transfor
mation_into_a_competitive_advantage_wp.pdf
35 https://www.okta.com/solutions/secure-ciam/

Since then their CIAM focused offering concentrates on the customer journey from acquisition, retention, personalisation and trust via privacy. They offer a cloud and hybrid on-premise delivered API first solution[36], covering registration, login, user storage, self service, MFA and standards based federation.

Origins within Marketing

A second angle to consider, are CIAM vendors that started to attack the capability set with a slightly different approach. As CIAM is directly contributing to revenue generation and user acquisition, many CIAM capabilities had their initial origins from a marketing landscape. The focus here was on identity registration–deep integrations, yet simple to configure–services that leveraged the social media identity providers such as Facebook, Twitter, Instagram and LinkedIn. By collapsing the complexity gap during user registration, many services could acquire new users faster.

Coupled to that, increased functionality in user analytics and reporting, allowed service owners to build a greater set of insights in how users register and use their offering. Questions such as "what are the triggers to registration?", "what causes abandoned shopping cart scenarios?", "what do the users do once they register?" and "what is driving engagement?" are fundamental to understanding how marketing focused campaigns for managing user acquisition are measured.

36https://www.pingidentity.com/en/solutions/customer-identity.html

Let us again take a look (in alphabetic order) of some sample vendors in the marketing based genus.

Akamai Technologies (formerly Janrain)

Akamai Technologies was founded in 1998 and is focused upon delivering cloud based content delivery and secure omnichannel experiences. In January 2019, they acquired Janrain[37], a cloud provider of CIAM technologies, which has now become the Akamai Identity Cloud[38]. Janrain's main focus was upon data harvesting–integrating with numerous data providers and social networks–to streamline the user acquisition process. Once registered Janrain provided a range of analytics capabilities focused on user breakdown (gender, demographics, age, likes) with the ability for the end user to export and manage their data in compliant ways.

LoginRadius

LoginRadius is a Canadian provider, founded in 2012, focused on delivering cloud based CIAM capabilities, split into two areas: Customer Experience[39] and Customer Trust[40]. Customer Experience is angled at delivering personalised user onboarding and login journeys, that are localised

37 https://www.akamai.com/us/en/about/news/press/2019-press/akamai-to-add-customer-identity-access-management-capability-to-enhance-digital-trust-by-acquiring-janrain.jsp
38 https://www.akamai.com/uk/en/products/security/identity-cloud.jsp
39 https://www.loginradius.com/customer-experience-solutions/
40 https://www.loginradius.com/customer-security/

and highly performant. Customer Trust is looking at the security and privacy feature space, by integrating consent related workflows. CIAM capability coverage in general covers web and mobile SSO, identity provider integration, user directory storage and progressive profiling, data governance and compliance and basic security constraints.

SAP Customer Data Cloud (formerly Gigya)

SAP is a German based enterprise resource planning provider, founded in the early 1970's, with a large multinational presence. As expected for a company of their size and longevity, they have made numerous acquisitions—over 40[41] by 2020. One of those acquisitions, was for a company called Gigya in 2017[42]. Gigya was rolled into SAP's Customer Data Cloud[43], where it delivers personalised business to consumer engagement capabilities, via a cloud based platform. Like many marketing focused solutions, rapid customer onboarding, consent management and analytics are the main focus. Other capabilities include strong data privacy and compliance to regulations such as GDPR and CCPA.

PaaS Big 3: "AmaGooMi"

With regards to PaaS delivered functionality, we will first

[41] https://www.crunchbase.com/organization/sap#section-acquisitions
[42] https://techcrunch.com/2017/09/24/sap-is-buying-identity-management-firm-gigya-for-350m/
[43] https://www.sap.com/uk/products/crm/customer-data-management.html

define the term PaaS, as meaning the delivery of a set of combined–often individually consumed–services, covering a range of different use cases. It is interesting to also note that these platforms are not solely focused on CIAM. The main three PaaS vendors we will discuss, likely require no introduction: Amazon, Google and Microsoft.

All three provide a range of differing and competing infrastructure, machine learning, security, big data and cloud computing resources, that power some of the internet's biggest applications and services.

With regards to the rise of CIAM related capabilities within the "AmaGooMi" group, the origin of functionality would sit under the IAM umbrella –namely foundational services for user authentication, identity storage, multi factor authentication and contextual authorization. Of course the capabilities offered by each provider are vast and ever expanding and would likely also cover analytics and data management too if the client wished to build them.

Amazon

Amazon Web Services provides an Identity and Access Management set of capabilities under the name of "Cognito"[44]. AWS Cognito offers an API first supported feature set, that covers user storage, identity federation for standards based integration–including social providers–and various different multi factor authentication options. The pricing tier goes to projects scaling 10 million plus

[44]https://aws.amazon.com/cognito/

users. The Cognito capabilities essentially provide user access to other resources within the AWS ecosystem, allowing a customer to build out a set of CIAM applications secured by Cognito. Application integration–for mobile for example–is accelerated by code samples and widgets. Whilst Cognito is not explicitly designed for CIAM, the capabilities overlap and complex feature sets can be architected together using their APIs.

Google

Google has a range of IAM capabilities and in 2018, announced a specific solution set called CICP[45]–Cloud Identity for Customers and Partners. As the name suggests, the focus was on protecting applications and resources, for users outside of the traditional organisational boundary. One of the key messages, is to apply "Google grade authentication"–powered by their Firebase[46] brand–to service provider applications, by leveraging SDKs (software development kits) for multiple different languages. Applications can also leverage threat intelligence tooling that can be used to identify scenarios where MFA is required. Another focus for Google seems to be on scalability. As described in the nonfunctional section on core capabilities, high volumes of active users and system throughput are likely in a CIAM solution and Google describes their support for this with "planet scale

45 https://cloud.google.com/blog/products/identity-security/cloud-identity-for-customers-and-partners-cicp-is-now-in-beta-and-ready-to-use
46 https://firebase.google.com/products/auth/

infrastructure".

Microsoft

Microsoft has provided enterprise grade IAM capabilities for nearly two decades, since the early incarnations of Active Directory (AD), which arrived with Windows 2000. Since then they have expanded in numerous directions, first by leveraging the power of AD within its Azure cloud ecosystem, and latterly by offering an Azure AD business to consumer solution[47]. Azure AD B2C focuses on four pillars: high availability and high scale, fine grained customization for registration, strong authentication options and data integration. Microsoft is also focusing heavily on the security angle of CIAM—with investment of $1 billion[48] a year on cyber security research, which can be leveraged within the Azure ecosystem, alongside numerous industry certifications for data security compliance.

Emergent Suppliers

So far in the discussion around the CIAM market breakdown, we have covered suppliers who have origins from orthogonal areas—namely employee IAM and marketing. There are, of course, more organic suppliers, who have emerged within the last seven years and are building capabilities primarily for the modern digital

47 https://azure.microsoft.com/en-gb/services/active-directory/external-identities/b2c/
48 https://azure.microsoft.com/en-gb/services/active-directory/external-identities/b2c/#security

landscape, where of course CIAM resides. Most modern digital identity systems are likely to be API, mobile and cloud ready, easy to scale and expand and are driven by solving two main issues: *usability* and *security*.

Digital identity can of course be well suited to both IAM and CIAM projects and many organisations who are undergoing digital transformation from an outside-in perspective, may also look to redesign internal employee and partner processes, systems and controls, in order to create a foundation where CIAM solutions can be developed.

Auth0

Auth0 was founded in 2013, headquartered in Washington (USA) and has received over $200m in venture funding[49] as of June 2020. The Auth0 solution is a cloud focused platform, that is developer-first in its design strategy, with support for multiple different language integrations, SDK's and code "widgets" to accelerate development. The core functionality covers a Universal Login, Single Sign On, MFA, Breached Password Detection, User Management, Passwordless and integration for Machine to Machine communications. The Auth0 pricing model[50], looks to differentiate between internal and external users.

49https://www.crunchbase.com/organization/auth0
50https://auth0.com/pricing/

Cloudentity

Cloudentity was founded in 2011[51] and is headquartered in Seattle, USA, and was formerly called Syntegrity. Cloudentity offers its microservices based solutions that focus upon delivering modern IAM related use cases—with a distinct focus on API powered CIAM. Its Digital Identity Plane[52] looks to power "business to business to consumer" services with self service, account linking, adaptive authentication, MFA and BYOID. Its Authorization Control Plane[53] centres around API protection, using modern standards, whilst integrating consent management and data normalization capabilities.

Idaptive

Idaptive is a cloud vendor, that was a spin off from privileged access management provider Centrify, back in 2018[54]. The spin off allowed Idaptive to focus on delivering zero trust enabled architectures that were strong on contextual and adaptive access. Whilst the initial focus seemed to be employee and partner lead ecosystems, clearly many CIAM solutions, rich in API first and digital currency, have trust and security at their core too. The Idaptive product set features capabilities within multi factor authentication, single sign on, provisioning and life

51 https://www.crunchbase.com/organization/syntegrity-networks
52 https://cloudentity.com/identity-management/
53 https://cloudentity.com/authorization-control/
54 https://www.centrify.com/about-us/news/press-releases/2018/centrify-spins-out-idaptive/

cycle management and endpoint and mobile security. The San Francisco based organisation was acquired by another privileged access management provider CyberArk in 2020[55].

Open Source

A final thought on vendors, concerns a brief mention for open source providers. Open source of course does not necessarily mean free, but it may mean more transparency, more freedom to customize and extend and be faster to test and develop against. Two vendors to mention in this space are Gluu and WS02. Gluu was founded in 2009 and is based in the United States. Its origins are focused on federation and access management, with multiple capabilities applicable to CIAM, including user managed access (UMA) as a Kantara Initiative focused on user centric access control and consent. WS02 is also headquartered in the USA, with multiple open source service bus and transformation components. The WS02 identity components provide support for scalable API protection amongst other features.

Market Breakdown Summary

In this section, we discussed some of the specialist commercial off the shelf providers in the CIAM space and how they typically ground their feature set, either from an employee IAM and security standpoint, or from a business

55 https://www.cyberark.com/resources/blog/the-time-is-now-cyberark-acquires-idaptive

enablement and marketing position. Clearly vendors from each background have now built capabilities across a range of CIAM use cases and overlap immensely between security and marketing.

Of the emergent suppliers, being mobile ready, API first and cloud delivered, seem standard modus operandi, allowing for rapid application onboarding and integration.

One final comment on that of costings–which we will revisit in a later chapter focused on vendor selection. Pricing for most vendors is typically a calculation based on the number of users and functionality integrated. In some cloud providers, nonfunctional costings can be expected too, typically centered around single -v- multi-tenant architectures if a pure cloud supplier, support response times and potentially some transaction or throughput style metering too.

For software that is typically deployed in private clouds via DevOps style models, costs need to be considered for delivery personnel–either directly employed as contractors or via third party system integrators.

In both private cloud and SaaS style settings, it is also common for consultancy–often focused on design, vendor selection and integration architecture.

Future Trends

Let us finish this chapter by spending some time on the potential future trends of CIAM capabilities and the role of CIAM suppliers over the coming 3-5 years. Analysis of any "future state" is complex, with multiple different factors to analyse before coming to a rational conclusion. Not only does this require analysing vast amounts of information, from a wide and varied set of data points, it also involves mapping those data points to any emerging trends–however weak they may seem.

Trends are often driven by basic human needs–such as the Maslow hierarchy[56]–which describes the building blocks of basic, physiological and psychology needs. Whilst clearly not created for the needs of digital identity and transformation, some interesting aspects of the Maslow hierarchy standout–namely the need for security, relationships and prestige. Those could easily be three powerful characteristics of a successful digital service, that delivers personalised user-centric experiences, that build trust.

Some other forces for changing trends, can be broken down into the simple PEST model–political, economic, social and technological. By grouping macro forces into these simple buckets allows us to capture any external factors that could impact organizational or vendor behaviour. For example, increased regulation by government policy for the handling of personal data, could

[56]https://en.wikipedia.org/wiki/Maslow%27s_hierarchy_of_needs

cause a rise in demand for privacy preserving technology.

Another example could be the economic changes resulting from the Covid-19 outbreak– requiring more flexible work from home arrangements, with online banking, retail and entertainment–causing demands for secure login and zero trust protection of APIs.

When it comes to understanding uncertainty, an organisation called the Future Today Institute[57] describes a concept called the "Axes of Uncertainty"[58], where you attempt to cross-map differing potential outcomes, in order to design appropriate responses–instead of reacting to change as it occurs. Let us take some examples of potential trends and attempt to see what outcomes could occur.

I want to break down the potential outcomes into three buckets: *convergence* of technology, the *commoditization* of features and the *conflict* of wants.

Convergence

Let us first look at technology convergence–the blurring together of different feature sets and even industries into one offering. Historical performance would indicate this is a relatively sound place for analysis, if we take examples such as the hardware convergence found in modern smartphones of a camera, torch, music player, telephone, internet browser, clock, alarm and so on. Other simple examples could include the bundling of infrastructure

[57] https://futuretodayinstitute.com/foresight-tools-2/
[58] https://futuretodayinstitute.com/mu_uploads/2020/04/Axes-FTI.pdf

services into the likes of Google Cloud Platform or Amazon Web Services, or how the TCP/IP stack, once a separate piece of software, is essentially a "free" part of any network attached device.

I want to focus on three orthogonal identity sectors and apply some concepts of *converged uncertainty*. Let us take a look at IAM, CIAM and PAM–privileged access management. Currently three distinct sectors, with different stakeholders and capabilities.

I am following the concept of "Axes of Uncertainty" in a vague sense, by taking four polarised outcomes and creating a 2 by 2 matrix. This provides one outcome of total convergence–where IAM, CIAM and PAM can be delivered and consumed in one flow. One outcome where IAM, CIAM and PAM start to actively diverge. The remaining two outcomes are hybrids.

The four resulting outcomes should hopefully provide some interesting discussion and thought processes around what might or might not happen, on both the supplier side through consolidation and converged offerings and from the buy-side, where use cases overlap and budgets become more blurred.

Figure 2.3 Converged Uncertainty for IAM, CIAM and PAM

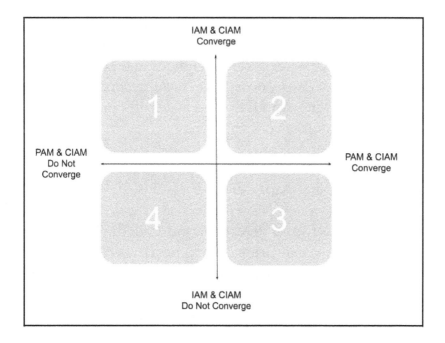

Let us break down the 4 outcomes, in clockwise order and add a brief explanation of the future state and potential impact.

1—IAM and CIAM Converge

Cause: Employees are consumers too and demand the same services, experiences and application patterns. Retail and online banking start to drive familiarity with user-centric digital journeys. Work patterns post Covid-19 also assumes a remote-first approach to accessing applications, requiring similar authentication and onboarding to consumers.

Effect: Persona based functionality allows easy splitting of roles on mobile and within applications for "Joe Bloggs employee" and "Joey the consumer". Shopping cart experiences for employees become standardised. End users within a CIAM ecosystem have access to identity governance-esque workflow to self-certify and allow 3rd party certification of verifiable claims.

2–IAM, CIAM and PAM Converge

Cause: As the rise of zero trust and CARTA (continuous adaptive risk and trust assessment) based security ecosystems for employees becomes standard, privileged access paradigms such as zero standing privileges and just in time provisioning become absorbed in all identity services.

Effect: Many redundant protection mechanisms start to become obsolete, as identity accounts become empty vehicles layered in crypto based authentication and event triggered access. Internally managed services and API's are essentially accessible from any public network, with authorization enforcement being done within applications or in contextually aware proxies and side cars.

3–CIAM and PAM Converge

Cause: The paradox of "privacy -v- personalisation" drives a need for temporal, privacy enriched consumer journeys that are backed by privileged access principles. The end user wants an ever more personal experience from the digital services they sign up for–yet compliance and regulation drive deeper requirements for privacy.

Effect: Personal Identifiable Information (PII) is essentially treated as a single protected sub-system with vaulted access requests and management. The use of crypto based storage for PII will be common, with access requests and usage, being transparently recorded and controlled.

4–IAM, CIAM and PAM Diverge

Cause: Consumers demand more personalised, seamless experiences that drive more disposable and pseudonymous identity services. Workforce enablement becomes fragmented, with organisations relying on complex supply chain integrations across different clouds. Zero trust drives specialised controls for privileged systems across hybrid locations too.

Effect: Further siloes and management of systems handling identity data within different ecosystems. Increased duplication of effort, management and operational controls, resulting in increased attack services and budget inefficiencies.

If the process of convergence takes hold, there will be many features, which will become essentially free or commodity and many may in fact become redundant

entirely.   Let   us   take   a   brief   look   at   feature
commoditization.

Commoditization

As with many market sectors, a level of commoditization of features and functions often occurs. This process[59], is often seen as a market moving towards (albeit not obtaining) a position of *perfect competition,* where the pricing power of a supplier weakens and the features they offer become *undifferentiated* in the eyes of the buyer. This allows the buyer to essentially move towards a position of having perfect information regarding supplier products, allowing them to make better decisions around fit and supply.

There are two main features of CIAM that could fall into this category: multi factor authentication (MFA) and passwordless authentication.   Both capabilities are important aspects of defining both a secure and usable set of security controls for both employee IAM and CIAM.

MFA fits into the umbrella of user authentication, which is typically split into three main categories: something you *know* (such as a PIN or password), something you *have* (like a security fob or key) and something you *are* (like a biometric print). The driver behind MFA is to create a user authentication event that aims to capture 2 of the three authentication categories.

Commoditization of MFA

59https://en.wikipedia.org/wiki/Commoditization

Cause: The ubiquitous nature of mobile phones and "apps", has allowed the development of one time password (OTP) generators being made freely available on the main app stores–namely Google Play and Apple App Store. These OTP generators typically support OATH (open authentication)[60] compliant ways of generating 6 digit pass codes. Coupled with that, many of the main social media sites such as Facebook, LinkedIn, Twitter and Google provide second factor capabilities based on authenticator apps, which drives awareness and uptake.

Effect: Due to the free nature of OTP generator apps–that are standards based–and the increased end user awareness and usage, MFA technology becomes a standard part of the CIAM login experience. End users are no longer inhibited by MFA and indeed expect it, if seeking a trusted end user journey.   Such basic MFA tooling, focused on OTP generation, may provide enough security for 80% of CIAM focused projects, with more specialised MFA solutions being limited to the remaining 20% where increased levels of friction and security may be required.

A relation to MFA, is that of passwordless, the deemed panacea of user based authentication across the board, regardless of whether employee or consumer related. Passwordless has the association with being dual beneficial–it can improve security via reducing data breaches associated with password theft or credential stuffing attacks–whilst simultaneously improving usability.

60https://openauthentication.org/

Commoditization of Passwordless

Cause: The increased focus on passwordless technology, resulted in a new standard being developed by the W3C, called WebAuthn[61]. This standard leverages capabilities built within modern versions of internet browsers to trigger logon events based on classic public key cryptography. The standard was worked on by the likes of Google, Mozilla, Microsoft, Yubico and Nok-Nok Labs and has gained traction since being ratified in 2019.

Coupled with a popular standardized approach, has been the continued rise in data breaches associated with identity and password data–with services such as HaveIBeenPwned[62] now listing over 9 billion pwned accounts as of June 2020. This helps amplify the message that passwords are inherently insecure.

Effect: Passwordless flows, especially for web based applications now moves towards being a simple integration event–without the need for proprietary technology. Being a standard too, shows a level of peer review has been completed, which can promote increased adoption, especially for sectors adhering to stricter controls.

Commoditization Summary

Over time, more capabilities will essentially become

61 https://www.w3.org/TR/webauthn/
62 https://haveibeenpwned.com/

commoditized and potentially "free" at the point of consumption—albeit the design, integration and ongoing support effort is likely to be still costly. Commoditization is likely to occur first at the edge of a delivered platform, where the feature becomes duplicated across similar providers of an unrelated technology. For example, if a CIAM specific piece of functionality became common across the "AmaGooMi" platforms (who if we recall, are not specialist CIAM providers), this may indicate that the feature is now an expected and omnipresent part of the delivery cycle, and that commoditization may have occurred.

We have covered two C's so far, in convergence and commoditization—let us finish this chapter with one more—that of feature *conflict*.

Conflict

I want us to discuss a major paradox at the heart of CIAM—the conflict between user personalisation and user privacy. The personalisation versus privacy discussion, really has its origins associated with a much deeper conflict—one which is applicable to all walks of digital computation—is that of *usability* versus *security*. Traditionally usability and security were at opposite ends of a small spectrum, where security controls were typically driven from the IT technical landscape. Success metrics for security where often associated with the "*prediction*", "*detection*" and "*response*" phases associated with breaches of the confidentiality, integrity and availability information security triad[63].

Security Metrics

The key performance indicators for security[64], were often associated with different areas related to process, infrastructure and people. Examples included

- What percentage of systems have had a risk assessment?
- What percentage of systems have had security control assessments?
- How many blocked inbound requests did the firewall capture?
- How many failed authentications did the web portal receive?
- What percentage of servers are patched within the last 2 service pack versions?
- What percentage of desktops are updated within the last 2 virus definition updates?
- What percentage of end users are enrolled for MFA?

Another angle on security metrics, is often associated with a concept called Time Based Security (TBS)[65]. TBS essentially focuses on a simple equation, used to analyse whether the existing security controls are effective and require re-investment.

63 https://en.wikipedia.org/wiki/Information_security#Key_concepts
64 https://owasp.org/www-pdf-archive/Security_Metics-_What_can_we_measure-_Zed_Abbadi.pdf
65 https://winnschwartau.com/wp-content/uploads/2019/06/TimeBasedSecurity.pdf

TBS describes effective security as being true, if:

$$Protection_{time} > (Detection_{time} + Reaction_{time})$$

Here, if the protection aspect–for example the time it takes to break past the login system–takes longer than the time it takes to *detect* a break in and then *react* and stop the break in taking place, you are "secure". If the equation doesn't hold, the attacker wins– either because they broke in and you didn't know, or you did know but couldn't react fast enough.

Whether your security metrics use traditional or TBS methods, many are not centered around user experience. They are focused on either technical controls or a monetary return on investments associated with risk reduction.

Usability Metrics

Usability on the other hand, is often driven by other parts of the business–perhaps marketing, business development or product management–where feedback on the *effectiveness*, *efficiency* and *satisfaction* of a system are of immediate concern. Usability metrics[66] suddenly generate a huge level of interest, for those launching an internet facing digital service or platform. Concepts such as abandoned shopping carts, self service success, customer acquisition,

66 https://usabilitygeek.com/usability-metrics-a-guide-to-quantify-system-usability/

customer retention and customer churn become the main focus of usability improvements.

So what sorts of things are we measuring when it comes to usability? Let us first define the main concepts of *effectiveness* (being the accuracy a task is completed), the *efficiency* (as being the resources and effort expended in completion of a task) and *satisfaction* (as focusing on the comfort and acceptability of use). We can then start to add measurability on to those three subtopics–with measurability being something that is both observable and relatively quantifiable.

Some basic examples of usability metrics could include:

- What percentage of tasks could be completed?
- What percentage of tasks were completed error free?
- How long did the task take to complete?
- How difficult was the task to complete?
- How satisfied was the end user once the task was completed?

Clearly usability will have varying levels of significance throughout the CIAM lifecycle–like most relationships in the physical world, the initial "first meet" with a digital service will create an expectation regarding future usage and the initial customer acquisition and onboarding component may receive the most effort when it comes to usability and design.

However, the entire customer lifecycle–from acquisition through to growth, retention, usage, trust building and renewal–can all result in negative experiences which impact net promoter scores and recommendations, if the usability is deemed to be poor.

So is there a future path that can satisfy both the security aspect and end user experience? Will a standard blended experience develop that can satisfy both audiences, that is repeatable and economic to implement?

Blended Experience

Clearly a blending of the two polar opposites is a logical goal–taking the essential components from both camps and merging in order to deliver modern digital experiences[67] that focus on personalisation, yet uphold the basic tenets of confidentiality, integrity and availability. Future platforms and providers will look to create a pattern for this deployment approach. But what will that look like?

67 https://www.mckinsey.com/business-functions/risk/our-insights/building-security-into-the-customer-experience

Figure 2.4 The blending of security and usability

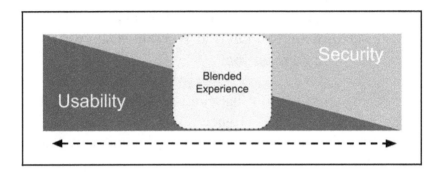

Persona Based

Firstly, not all users of a CIAM system will be the same. Coarse grained demographics would indicate age, gender and location metrics will vary widely, indicating subtle requirements in how systems are designed. Coupled with that, there are likely to be different personas associated with the service features, lifecycle and usage. For example, personas could exist for high frequency early adopters or market laggards who enroll once a level of feature maturity has been reached.

By identifying different user demographics and personas, usability changes can be much more focused. For example, a password reset service used by infrequent users of the service, who are aged over 60 and primarily use laptops, would create different requirements to an under 30 active user who accessed the system primarily via mobile.

Personas can also assist in building behaviour patterns that can help consolidate security controls and accelerate anomaly detection.

Offer Choice

Personas also facilitate another feature, which is that of increased choice. Choice works in two ways: choice for the end user and choice for the provider. From an end user perspective choice will appear at various points of the CIAM lifecycle. During login for example, choice could be used to provide flexible options regarding MFA selection. Not all MFA modals are the same and by providing a simple element of choice regarding whether a user wants to use a one time password, biometric or push notification for example, can greatly aid delivering a personalised experience.

Choice of course can also be applied on the CIAM provider side too–by allowing flexible configuration and selection of features, integration options, MFA modals and so on. Choice of integration is likely to move towards a business as usual activity, where agility and rapid change become standard, no longer requiring waterfall[68] design and implementation approaches.

Event Driven

The process of mapping personas can also be extended to persona-journeys and events within the CIAM lifecycle. Events could be simple and pre-designed such as registration via a specific social provider, a progressive

68 https://en.wikipedia.org/wiki/Waterfall_model

registration trigger, MFA enrollment or high risk transaction processing. Service specific events could include things like usage patterns, loyalty rewards, behaviour analytics and so on, that alter the service response, or trigger enhanced security checking. Within each event, a control posture and usability metric would exist, with a blend of the two being used to select the optimum modern CIAM experience.

Adaptive

Events themselves, will be numerous and sometimes complex, perhaps being combined together in order to form user journeys. Each journey will take numerous different steps to complete, often with context driving which response the service should arrive at. For example, a journey that is designed to capture the end user acceptance of new terms and conditions, may deliver the terms only when the user is on a laptop device (which provides a better reading experience), outside of work hours (where concentration may be distracted) and after 7pm when the user may be relaxing and not in a hurry somewhere. Each of those nuanced pieces of context, will allow the service to deliver an adaptive experience.

Another example, and one which takes user actions into consideration, is often associated with high risk event processing. A high risk event, could be something like changing the address on an account that is only 3 months old. This is a user triggered event, but could easily be used maliciously via an account takeover attack, where goods or services are sought to be delivered to a location unknown to the true account holder. In this case, the service provider needs to apply security controls in an adaptive way—preventing the bad, but also allowing the good—where genuine changes of address need to be clearly identified in a way which doesn't excessively inhibit the user journey.

Let us finish this section with some concrete examples of a potential future state blended experience.

Figure 2.5 Future state blended experience examples

Event	Persona	Blended Adaptive Response
Password reset policy	High frequency user, 100% mobile, early technology adopter	Provide choice regarding authentication options limiting to WebAuthn, OTP, push notification, in order to remove reliance on password entirely
	Low frequency user, 80% laptop, age > 60	Requirement of complex password, with support for password manager vaulting, with incentivised adoption of MFA—eg increased loyalty

		points.
Trusted device binding	User with more than 3 months history since registration, using same device	Bind device profile to the user's identity in order to reduce interruption during login and reduce need for MFA
	Brand new user credentials seen on 3 devices within 24 hours	Trigger extra security checking, MFA, auditing and device analysis
High risk transaction processing	User with 3 months worth of usage behaviour, on same device performing previously completed transaction, but in different location	Analyse behaviour and context, allowing event completion, with notification to end user to verify if indeed same user
	User with < 1 month usage, performing transaction for first time on new device	Analyse behaviour and context, allowing process completion, only after an MFA event has successfully completed on separate device

The conflicts within a CIAM landscape will be numerous, from usability versus security, through to the more subtle personalisation versus privacy and inconvenience versus trust.

Future CIAM suppliers will need to weave together capabilities and functions that operate on both sides of those conflicts, in order to deliver engaged user experiences.

Summary

This chapter focused on covering some of the existing suppliers and approaches to delivering CIAM solutions. We covered the main CIAM capabilities and how they somewhat overlap and differ from existing employee IAM projects. The market for CIAM providers is now large and varied, with the origins of many providers falling under a marketing or business enablement umbrella, or that of a more security and employee IAM foundation.

We briefly analysed some of the sample vendors in the space before taking a look at what the future for CIAM may look like, with a focus on the convergence of employee IAM, CIAM and privileged access management.

The conflicts in capabilities that CIAM can also be seen as a trigger for change and innovation in how digital solutions will evolve.

CHAPTER 3

CIAM Requirements

This chapter will focus upon some of the key requirements of a CIAM project, typically found under the umbrella of digital transformation and service transformation. The requirements for CIAM will often be split between the end user and the service provider, driven by trends in the external narrative, focused on changing consumer habits, technological advances, regulation & compliance and competitive market forces.

Many CIAM interactions will have bidirectional sets of flow—some originating from the end user, coming inbound, some originating from the service provider, going outbound. Some focused upon raw data, others more subtle and aimed towards personalised experience and seamless, yet adaptive interactions. But the first of any CIAM project is really the processing of getting to know your customer (or user).

Getting to Know Your Customers

The industry focus upon knowing your customer (KYC) is typically embedded within the process of performing due diligence upon an entity—typically a person—that is likely to be engaged in various financial transactions. We will cover this aspect momentarily, but often many CIAM projects will not be directly involved in monetary events, so we will expand the KYC concept to a few more areas–namely the *behaviour* and *personalisation* properties of each user of a system.

Not all users are created equally of course and those subtle differences in usage, behaviour and ultimately expectations, help the service provider not only deliver an improved service, but also to deliver a service that operates uniquely to a particular user's habits–the exact same way a physical interaction would occur.

AML

AML stands for anti money laundering. This is a process of ensuring the correct and legitimate processing of financial payments. AML is typically a legal requirement[69] for organisations that manage the processing of monetary transactions–from estate agents, lawyers and bookmakers, through to financial advisors and casino operators. Associations of this ilk, likely have to register[70] to a regional authority that handles regulation and governance of their particular sector. The main premise is to identify illegally obtained funds and how to prevent those funds from appearing to come from legitimate sources.

Many AML processes are upheld by legal regulation. Compliance against those regulations is a controlled and managed process. Regulators for each sector typical provide checklists[71] which can help organisations manage their internal status regarding AML compliance.

[69]http://www.legislation.gov.uk/uksi/2019/1511/contents/made

[70]https://www.gov.uk/anti-money-laundering-registration
[71]https://www.ifa.org.uk/media/853109/AML-compliance-checklist-final-060618.pdf

AML can be broken down into some clear areas, namely focused upon customer due diligence. Due diligence typically can be described as "taking steps to identify your customers and checking they are who they say they are."[72] The details of those "checks" will vary from country to country and industry to industry.

A common characteristic of initial customer due diligence, is the verification of identity based on previously issued credentials. This is the classic "show me your ID" use case—where the ID aspect is typically a government issued document such as a passport or driving license.

When the due diligence process takes place will vary—perhaps at the start of the business relationship dependent on the sector, or perhaps during a transaction that is seen to be unusual or above a certain threshold. It may also occur in a time based fashion—when the periodic checking of identity information is needed due to changes in personal circumstance and risk identification.

Due diligence isn't limited to basic identity verification though. So-called "enhanced" due diligence may also be triggered if initial checks were not satisfactory—perhaps where government issued documents could not be verified, or were from locations deemed a high risk.

Clearly in a physical setting, the showing of an ID card or passport within for example, a branch of a casino or retail bank is a pretty common, well understood and simple process. But how can that process be translated to an entirely digital setting? Obviously there are differences—in both usability and the security aspects too which we will

[72]https://www.gov.uk/guidance/money-laundering-regulations-your-responsibilities

cover in later sections.

There will be multiple other aspects to AML, that go above and beyond the due diligence aspect, that address things like business process, controls and the ongoing monitoring of the organisation, where the CIAM system may partake a roll–certainly around auditing and reporting–but the initial due diligence aspect would have some pretty strong overlap with the customer acquisition, retention and usage capabilities of a CIAM system.

* ★ Become aware of regional and sector specific AML compliance
* ★ Identify due diligence touch points
* ★ Develop automated processes

Fraud

A cousin to AML, is that of fraud. Fraud can be focused on both the internal and external business operational landscape–with attacks coming from both insider employees and external users of a system. We will focus on the latter, which fits in the CIAM narrative.

Externally generated fraud can occur at multiple points of an internet facing system and is not always related to monetary transactions. Fraudulent actors however, are typically motivated by monetary gain as an ultimate end goal, but the various stages to the fraud journey may include tactics touching the registration of fake accounts, attacks against rewards and loyalty systems, false reviews, automated recommendations and more. Like most criminal activities, fraud is driven by a *motivation*, an *opportunity* and a *rationalisation* of behaviour.

Figure 3.1 Example fraud attacks and associated business impact

Attack	Details	Cost	Mitigation
Business Email Compromise	Crafted email and spoofed sender	Data loss	Training; Monitoring; Reporting
Synthetic Registration	Mix of real and fake identity data during registration	Distorted analytics; Increased licensing/inf rastructure	Secure Customer Authenticati on; generic MFA; reCAPTCH A
Automated Activity (bot)	Post account creation automated logins and usage	Distorted analytics; Reputation;	Behaviour monitoring; Adaptive access
Transaction Fraud	Use of real identity in malicious scenario	Profit/Loss bottom line; Reputation; Compliance	Behaviour monitoring; Step Up MFA
Call Centre Identity Fraud	Use of real identity in malicious scenario	Profit/Loss bottom line; Reputation; Compliance	Voice biometrics; Out of band authenticati on

Fraud is likely to be experienced by all sectors and verticals and not just those services focused upon monetary events like AML compliance would be. Fraud management is also not as highly regulated, with protection, detection and management systems being deployed more from an operational standpoint to help reduce the *cost* of fraud.

Fraud systems can typically fall into two main areas: niche fraud detection and fraud management. The nuance between the two is subtle, with management being a more generic umbrella looking at the end to end lifecycle of fraud control–covering the typical information security pillars of protection, detection and response. Response in a fraud culture could be wide and varied–from disrupting and stopping a particular event and transaction, right through to forensic analysis and investigation that results in policy changes or system rule changes.

Fraud management in general can be overlaid against multiple parts of the CIAM lifecycle–from registration events, usage and behaviour analysis, through to high value transactions processing, referral and service recommendation. All could be attacked using fraudulent tools, techniques and procedures.

- ★ Leverage protection, detection and response management tooling
- ★ Apply fraud management to all parts of CIAM lifecycle
- ★ Analyse feedback based on forensic investigation

Fraud Detection

Detection is essentially the identification of anomalies in a timely fashion. In *chapter 2* we briefly touched on Time Based Security, where the timeliness of the detection (and ultimately response) are critical to ensuring your controls are effective and provide a clear return on investment. Fraud detection can also be something of a paradox. If the sole purpose is to identify anomalous activity, which in turn can help build trust within the service for the end user, the detection aspect needs to be completed without unnecessarily inhibiting real user activity. That last point is significant. If a high number of "real" events get blocked on suspicion of fraud, suddenly the user experience degradation can have a larger impact than the reputational damage and financial cost associated with actual fraudulent activity. This brings us to the classic "crossover error"[73] rate problem–where the false reject rate (FRR)–real user events, seen as fraudulent– is minimised in comparison to the false accept rate (FAR), where fraudulent events are let through. As with any anomaly detection, the definition of "normal" needs to be created with the ability to identify deviations from this, either for individuals or groups of individuals. Data science and machine learning is likely to have a strong foothold in these systems.

Fraud Management

Fraud management is typically an overarching term focused on the generic three pillars of information security, namely protect, detect, respond. The aspects of fraud response (especially with regard to internal employee focused fraud) are often managed by fraud response[74] plans. The plan is a documented way to articulate both internally and externally, the process, steps and accountable parties in the

[73]https://www.sciencedirect.com/topics/computer-science/crossover-error-rate
[74]https://www.cimaglobal.com/Documents/ImportedDocuments/
cid_techguide_fraud_risk_management_feb09.pdf.pdf

117

response to identified fraud or suspected fraud. In many regulated industries the public notification process is often compulsory, requiring detailed and timely communications to members, consumers, stakeholders and regulatory offices. With specific focus on a CIAM system, the response could well include multiple changes to technical controls (for example registration or login events) as well as auditing, monitoring and usability. The tooling required in order to make such granular changes, is likely to focus on fraud case management, evidence capture and storage, forensic analysis and process replay.

So far we have focused our discussion on some high level control focused touch points when it comes to getting to know your members or users. AML and fraud are critical, but there are some other areas we should explore too.

Behaviour

User behaviour is a broad and varied topic. Many fraud and AML systems will use behaviour profiles for specific journeys in order to identify differences and anomalous activity. However, we need to expand the focus within CIAM in order to identify patterns of behaviour at multiple parts of the user lifecycle. We will devote an entire chapter to the CIAM lifecycle later in the book, but we can now start to think a little of CIAM as being part of a cycle. That cycle will contain various distinct phases such as user acquisition, usage, renewal and so on. Each of those phases will in turn contain multiple events which join to create journeys. The behaviour of the "one and many" within those journeys will be critical in driving usability, security and ultimately the success of the CIAM core.

Figure 3.2 Behaviour as a "cog" within the CIAM life cycle

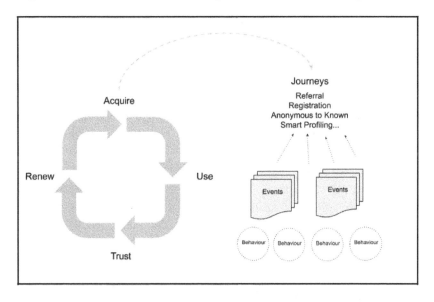

Figure 3.2 shows how basic behaviour analysis is likely to occur at multiple parts of the CIAM life cycle, within specific journeys and likely on events within those journeys. For example, why an individual chooses to use push authentication or a one time password sent via email, may be driven by location, phone type or network operator. It may also be due to a poor push network operator that doesn't always deliver the message, or perhaps the feature is confusing to set up. Knowing the nuanced differences, helps to improve security and also prevent unnecessary interruptions or options.

Drivers, barriers & hooks

By being able to identify patterns is critical for several reasons. From a pure conversion and acquisition perspective, there are typically three main steps of analysis to delivering a digital service

119

that is engaging and delivers value. There are typically the *drivers*, *barriers* and *hooks*[75] that exist within your system. The drivers are the flows that are pushing users to your system. The barriers are components, features or steps that are either driving users away, or preventing them from completing a task with a degree of satisfaction. Hooks are typically steps that persuade a user to change behaviour in a positive way. By analysing behaviour at each of those three main steps, you can have a significant impact on usability and conversion. Small changes can have a large impact. For example, by making small changes to the multi-factor authentication (MFA) registration and usage events, could have a huge impact on the user registration journey and in turn conversion rates.

If it bleeds we can kill it

"If it bleeds we can kill it" is a rather crude quote taken from the 1987 film "Predator". The analogy refers to the point, that if something is measurable, it can be improved upon. By taking the basic three steps of behaviour analysis and applying some analytical techniques, the CIAM system can be tuned to a point where unnecessary questions are removed, unnecessary assumptions are avoided and end users can be sent into funnels of behaviour that improve usability and security. The behaviour analysis process should include both simple yet measurable metrics that can be tied to changes, either positive or negative with regards to user interactions.

75https://www.hotjar.com/conversion-rate-optimization/cro-program/

Measure, iterate, then measure again

Some basic examples of event analysis could include session recording or monitoring (with the appropriate levels of consent of course), heat maps of interaction (seeing where users spend most of their time on a page or feature) or even basic surveys and question interruptions. You could articulate those analytical techniques as being quite active. A more passive set of techniques could include looking at meters and timers based on interactions. A simple example could include monitoring how long a new biometric MFA event takes in comparison to a simple one time password. Those times could be correlated to abandoned shopping cart (or non-monetary equivalent) events to identify any cross correlation. The more "passive" measurements are also likely within A/B testing scenarios, where two distinct options are presented to the user with meters and timers used to track outcomes.

★ Develop journeys and event stories to track behaviour
★ Measure and quantify individual steps
★ Create hypotheses, test and iterate

Figure 3.4 Example CIAM behaviour analysis touch points

Event/Journey	Analysis Type	Outcome
Primary registration device & location	Metering	Knowledge of geo-locations to device type, OS and browser

		version for support
Credential reset	Heatmap; timers	Ability to reduce call centre contact time
MFA enrollment	Metering; timers; questions	Identify most preferred modals and methods; help reduce support matrix and attack vectors
Initial registration	Heatmaps, timers, questions	Streamlined onboarding experience
Transaction payment	Past and peer behaviour comparison	Increased security; reduced interruptions

In this section we have covered a few areas focused on analysing user actions. Let us dive into how that information can be used to drive one key part of a digital CIAM experience—that of personalisation.

Personalisation

Personalisation is akin to the comedy panacea of being able to keep everyone happy, all of the time. As John Lydgate said "You can please some of the people all of the time, you can please all of the people some of the time, but you can't please all of the people all of the time" It's a tough challenge. Any website or application aims to deliver a service or content to an often highly distributed, opinionated and educated end user community. How to keep all of them engaged, informed and empowered, all of the time? Well, it may be a hard challenge, but personalised experiences can go some way to help.

How?

Humanise, Offer Choice & Predict

The first part of the personalisation journey is to start *humanizing* relations with the end user. They are no long "users", "customers", "consumers" or "clients". Treat them instead, like partners, members or even human beings! For example, even before a login event has occurred, if the person has used your system previously, a persistent cookie or other seamless method of pre-authentication can simply provide a "Welcome back Simon" message or similar label. Instantly, that can bring a softening to the initial interaction. Even on areas where authentication has not occurred, the use of terminology and concepts taken from the physical world can help to create a more human-centric experience.

- ★ Use terms such as members or partners
- ★ Use given names
- ★ Authenticate interactions–even if need improving

A classic aspect of physical human interactions is that of *choice*. The amount of choice available in the standard coffee shop[76] is astounding. Coffee is no longer coffee. Every coffee drinker has their own nuanced specialist likes

---

76 https://www.starbucks.com/menu/drinks/hot-coffees

and preferences. A coffee shop owner can capture more marginal revenue by offering more choice, as long as this doesn't negatively affect cost. In a digital setting, the ability to ask, capture and quantify user feedback can provide bi-directional benefits. Firstly the user feels listened to, if you offer choice. You can trigger a feeling of *digital empathy* by asking questions and understanding the reasons behind user behaviour. Does the user want to enable MFA? If they do perhaps their subscription cost might be lower. Would they like to use push authentication, a one time password or voice biometric? Three relatively basic options, but each one likely to generate different responses to different people under different circumstances. By being able to capture personal preference can help build trust and improve user experience.

★ Replicate physical choice
★ Ask, prompt and capture
★ Generate digital empathy

A *prediction* aspect also helps with respect to humanising and is powered by the previous choices the user has made. It can help on two fronts: firstly to assist and help someone navigate a system better, by nudging and guiding behaviour, but secondly, shows the system has listening and is responding. The prediction aspect is clearly dependent (and highly correlated) to the amount of data the service can leverage against the end user. We touched on the conflict between usability and security in *chapter 2* and we will cover the subtlety between privacy and personalisation later in this chapter, but it is worth noting that this conflict exists and needs to be effectively navigated. A simple prediction example, could be that since the end user is logging in from a mobile device at 745am, it is likely they're commuting to a place of work, and since their preference under these conditions is to use an MFA powered by a local fingerprint scan on their device, that is the presented login option.

- ★ Nudge and funnel
- ★ Predict, but allow exception handling
- ★ Show learnings

Reduce

Raymond Loewy[77] was an industrial designer who coined the termed MAYA–most advanced yet acceptable. He spent most of his career re-designing some of the most iconic brands and objects in America–from the Coca Cola bottle and the Greyhound bus through to Air Force 1. A main premise he had was to not only advance the object to a level of acceptable innovation, but to streamline, reduce, and declutter–allowing the object's true form to be amplified. The same can be true of CIAM life cycle interactions.

Clearly the onboarding and registration experience is of vital importance–too many barriers to adoption, too many decisions to be made, too many steps to complete–will simply result in frustrated and jaded users who will fail to

[77] https://www.raymondloewy.com/about/biography/

engage with your product or service, irregardless of how good it is. Reduction should really apply to all parts of the CIAM interaction. By removing decision points, mistakes can be minimised and complexity avoided. Smart profiling–where the service only collects granular pieces of information as they are needed–is a good basic example of reduction. This removes the ominous full page form filling of personal details, and replaces it with micro-interruptions that collect pertinent information as needed–with the reasons for capture being fully explained.

★ Declutter and remove unnecessary interruptions
★ Collect only pertinent data
★ Leverage choice and captured information

Be Continuous, Be Seamless

Many digital interactions are likely to occur over extended periods of time. Think for example, watching a box set, reading a newspaper, making a purchase or filing a tax return. All of those tasks are likely to take anything from an hour to several days. The process of starting and stopping should be entirely seamless. There is likely no concept of "logging off" as there is on a work PC. Someone may start their tax return at 5pm on a Friday evening and then continue on Sunday afternoon, simply by leaving their browser open. Can the back end service continue their session securely? Can the session be terminated and restarted? Does the user have to re-login? Can that login process be performed transparently? The continuous nature of online interactions must also cater for different devices. We will cover multi-platform journeys shortly, but continuous interactions must consider the start and finishing of a transaction on different devices–without interruptions that could derail or distract the process.

* ★ Consider scenarios and journeys that are long in duration
* ★ Consider scenarios that are likely to spontaneously stop
* ★ Consider scenario start and finishing steps on different devices

Data on Demand

Let us move on a gear and start to focus on data management requirements–an underlying goal of many online systems. We need to start thinking, what is CIAM really trying to achieve? If we abstract away the feature related capabilities such as authentication, registration and MFA, CIAM is really the layer that allows *people* to perform *tasks* online–in a secure and usable way.

Those tasks could be as simple as getting a quote for car insurance, through to booking medical care or paying income tax. Some functions will be complex, others simple and intuitive. The consistent element is that of *data*. Data that is being generated. Data that is being shared. Data that is being used. It is very likely in most scenarios data needs to be accessed–by the right people at the right time.

Data Lifecycle

This lifecycle is inspired a little by the Securosis Data Security Lifecycle[78] that was created back in 2007 by the Securosis analyst firm. The life cycle of data of any sort—CIAM related, cloud related or otherwise—certainly follows a cyclical pattern. I don't want to get too bogged down in data types right now—we'll cover data typing in another life cycle, that of the CIAM life cycle—in a later chapter. I do want to emphasise the multiple stages in data creation and deletion, and the necessary controls that a CIAM system will need to focus upon.

Why & How

Generating

Data clearly needs to be generated or created. In the lens of CIAM, the assumption is the data will either be created by, or associated to, a physical person such as PII, or relates to a person's activity within a particular system—such as media viewing, shopping or transaction data. Both classifications of data need to be handled in different ways, with clear pipelines focusing on how the data was created, the level of required authenticity associated with its creation, how it should be stored, accessed and processed. We will cover compliance requirements in later sections, but it's important to be aware of what local or sectoral compliance requirements that may apply during the initial creation process.

[78]https://securosis.com/blog/the-data-security-lifecycle-beta-1

The creation of PII related data, typically occurs during registration or onboarding. It may be captured via forms or manual entry, with additional attributes harvested from third party identity providers such as social media sites. Additional correlation of more corroborated data may also occur form internally verified systems–adding in data such as recent postal addresses.

Activity data will vary considerably from system to system and will also vary in quality and value. Activity data will likely generate integrations with third party data processing ecosystems, often spawning sub industries. Consent and data privacy mechanisms are likely in such ecosystems, where habits, transactions and system behaviour data is often cross pollinated with over social meta information in order to drive deep personalised responses and ultimately revenue generation via targeted services.

★ Understand sectoral and geographic data processing and compliance requirements
★ Model against need to know–collecting only what is essential
★ Classify data into persistent PII versus activity

Sharing

It is highly likely that data that has either been created, collected or aggregated is going to end up being shared in some capacity. It is clear that any data sharing must take place under the umbrella of the necessary compliance requirements such as the GDPR or CCPA. There are several aspects to consider when developing sharing systems–typically focused on the *who*, the *what*, the *why* and the *when*. In typical system-centric sharing mechanisms, the main *why* is executed by system administrators. They decide to share a folder to a particular group, or they provide access to a database table to an application or user. Access control policies are created and maintained.

In a CIAM environment however, the main sharing mechanism may well be initiated and executed by a non-technical end user. The sharing of photos to a printing service or the sharing of fitness and health metrics to an online weight loss application. Basic examples where the sharing apparatus is being driven by a standard user of the system–not an administrator. What challenges does that bring? Are the existing technical capabilities and standards appropriate? Are the end users technically capable to make informed decisions regarding data sharing? Are the implications of sharing data to other individuals and systems known?

  ★ Consider models where the end user is making sharing decisions
  ★ Make sure the implications of data sharing is understood by all parties
  ★ Is the user (aka data owner) aware of all sharing actions that have taken place?

Accessing

The act of sharing something, will trigger subsequent access events, either by other individuals or first and third party systems. Those access events need to occur in a secure and timely fashion, with the necessary audit and notification constructs in place. If I share my park run information to a third party fitness website, what exactly is shared? What will the data be used for? Is the access time bound and if so will it be revoked after a specified time period? If not time bound, can the original sharer subsequently revoke access? Revocation is also an interesting topic. It can be quite simple to revoke dynamic and ever changing information–for example stopping the upload of run and fitness information after a certain date to the fitness website. Subsequent runs won't be uploaded. But what about more static information? If, for example, I share my date of birth, that only needs sharing once–the information wont change and can be easily copied and stored by others.

Another requirement with data access, is that of implicit sharing. If Joe shares a photo to Bob, can Bob share that photo with Jenny? If they do, does Joe get notified? If Joe is notified can he revoke access? If Joe revokes access to Bob is access also revoked for Jenny?

- ★ Consider how shared data is accessed and what constraints should be put in place
- ★ Does implicit sharing exist within your ecosystem?
- ★ Do the necessary data access revocation processes exist?

When

Data in Motion

Data will typically need to move from one place to another. In the CIAM world those places are likely to be consuming applications—web interfaces and mobile applications —and backend services such as microservices, API's and web applications. Clearly a security first mind set should be applied regardless of whether the data is part of a CIAM project or not, but CIAM requirements often bring different challenges. The data involved may likely be of a personal nature, be transported to different devices—which we'll touch upon shortly—and accessible by a large third party ecosystem or supply chain. Application to application security is one concern—leveraging cryptography to not only authenticate applications themselves, but also provide network layer protection via the likes of TLS (transport layer security).

Figure 3.5 Example application data fulfillment

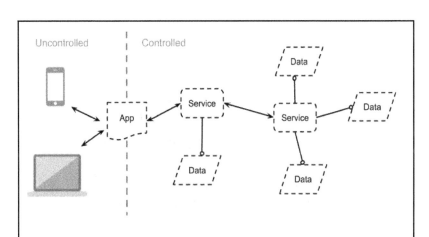

Figure 3.5 shows a basic example of the data in motion pipelines that need to be considered. The application may be controlled and built by an organisation, but the device and install process will not be. The underlying service to service integration will be controlled, but that is not to say it is protected from publicly accessible networks. Application assurance and service to service assurance and basic authentication and authorization controls should be in place.

★ Consider control boundaries and areas of data exposure
★ Application assurance and authentication needs to be factored
★ Service to service interactions should enforce authN, authZ and encryption

Data at Rest

The main requirement regarding CIAM data at rest, is what the data may contain. Clearly within the consumer world, PII, activity data and usage data may all well be part of the application and transport ecosystem. Where does that data reside at rest? On premise systems? Cloud systems controlled via platforms as a service (PaaS), rented infrastructure (Infrastructure as a Service, IaaS) or within third party systems (software as a service, SaaS)? The shared responsibility profile for each of those locations will be different. The control aspect as described in *figure 3.5* will also be different, governing what measures can be taken when and by whom. Data classification and tagging as well as the standard Data Privacy Impact Assessment[79] (DPIA) style work should be carried out if working with EU based users, in order to ascertain what data is stored where, and what controls need putting in place. Basic controls are likely to focus upon encryption, potential tokenization and entire removal of sensitive fields as well as controls centered around backup and recovery processes. Data retention may also impact some controls, as retention may last for several years, requiring long term encryption and key rotation considerations.

★ Identify, classify and tag CIAM related data
★ Identity a data shared responsibility model if working with off-premise locations

[79] https://ico.org.uk/for-organisations/guide-to-data-protection/guide-to-the-general-data-protection-regulation-gdpr/accountability-and-governance/data-protection-impact-assessments/

* DPIA's are a key component of GDPR (and other compliance) requirements

Data in Use

Data in use is often a forgotten about concept. This really refers to the runtime use of data to fulfill user or background application execution. Things to consider here focus around fail-safe and fail-open style scenarios as well as the necessary auditing and tracking of changes to analyse anomalous behaviour and unusual activity. Activity itself will be thoroughly guarded via the necessary authentication and access control mechanisms—either basic role based access, or more contextual attribute based access.

Data in use considerations could start within the applications themselves, with concepts such as runtime application self-protection (RASP)[80], right through to monitoring and management at the data persistence layer, such as making sure writes to a database are completed and result in consistent and replicated storage for example.

* Consider data change classifications—who (person or service) is expected to change what, when and how?
* Identify mechanisms to baseline data change events
* Consider what happens during data change failures—what does failure look like and how to implement resilience

---

80https://en.wikipedia.org/wiki/Runtime_application_self-protection

Any X - Location, Time & Device

The modern consumer will expect data on a device of their choosing, at a time convenient to them, without having to search for it. The data needs to find them, not the other way around. This creates the cyclical paradox of how to deliver usable, personalized and predictive experiences, whilst upholding security and privacy?

The areas of control for a service leader delivering a CIAM set of capabilities starts to diminish from both the application accessibility point, as well as the backend service fulfilment angle. By leveraging more cloud or third party services, may accelerate initial development, but also requires a deeper understanding of shared responsibility, especially with regards to data management.

From an application consumption perspective, the control often seen within an employee management desktop environment dissolves, with consumer facing web and mobile applications accessible from a myriad of device types, operating systems, browser versions, languages and locales. The support, testing and management of a web first ecosystem becomes complex, which can in turn create new attack vectors and usability headaches.

Multi-platform Journeys

Let us expand the "Any-X" paradigm now, and focus on the device landscape–from what will the typical CIAM user access your services and applications? Firstly, there probably isn't a typical user profile, and if there is, it will constantly change. What *is* consistent is change and variety. Remember a CIAM powered service is going to be internet facing–and that will bring variance and also opportunity.

Device Types

The What

First, let us take a look at what device types a CIAM system may need to provide services and functions for.

Mobile

Mobile first is a clear strategy for most organisations, regardless of whether that is driven by CIAM needs or not. Mobile has overtaken[81] desktop as the largest global device used on the internet and coupled with that, the ever present nature of a user to smartphone relationship, developing systems that are easily consumable via mobile seems a sensible initial step. But the mobile device–smart or otherwise–is not always the consuming device of the service. Many mobile interactions with a service often started off as a secondary or out of band device, typically used during authentication.

81https://gs.statcounter.com/platform-market-share/desktop-mobile-tablet

Figure 3.6 The changing role of mobile during authentication

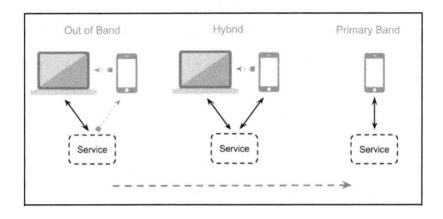

In an out of band scenario, the mobile is not consuming a service, merely providing extra functionality, typically seen during login. An evolution to that, or perhaps in parallel but within the enterprise space, came the concept of managing the device–perhaps via mobile device management[82] or enterprise mobile management solutions. Here, the level of assurance of the device increased, due to context checks, device authentication–often via public key cryptography (PKI) and application configuration guarantees. As a result, the device became trusted enough to start interacting with a backend service directly in its own right. The final step is simply one where all interactions occur over a single device. This alters the login flows substantially and may open up questions around a lack of security within the device itself, especially if the device is locked only by means of a simple PIN.

82https://en.wikipedia.org/wiki/Mobile_device_management

A CIAM ecosystem is likely to have to cater for all three scenarios–the hybrid one likely to be more subtle. Clearly in a CIAM world, the devices themselves would fall under a bring your own device (BYOD) flow, where pseudo control would merely come from software development kit (SDK) functionality that leverages mobile operating system features for checking device metadata, jailbreak status and other contextual information.

★ Develop with the assumption that mobile could be the only avenue of access
★ Consider security and privacy of mobile only interactions
★ Provide choice for hybrid and phone-as-a-token journeys

Laptop

Let us not forget about the laptop (or even desktop) too soon. For some scenarios a mobile device may not be entirely suitable. Initial registration for example, or the uploading and proofing of identity documents, the viewing of terms and conditions and billing information, or the raising of support tickets–may all benefit from a larger screen and full layout keyboard a laptop can offer. This brings several points that we touched upon during the personalisation topic–namely being able to continuously deliver a service, to multiple devices simultaneously–often with the start and end being on different devices.

The end user will expect the journey to be similar—if not the same—across devices, with the necessary information being instantly available, often with notifications across devices. A change in status for example being pushed to a mobile via an app notification. The ability to call the help desk and for them to instantly tie a telephone number to an identity, and then to the raised ticket and then to the status. Those nuanced pieces of context, allow touch points to become more seamless—but all require CIAM to be working effectively. *Figure 3.7* shows a basic multi-device, multi-touch journey. There are many examples, especially where devices are used for different tasks at different times. The mobile may switch from being used as an out of band authentication device, a device for reading a message, through to actually being used as a telephone to provide feedback on the call centre experience.

Figure 3.7 Example cross device continuous service journey

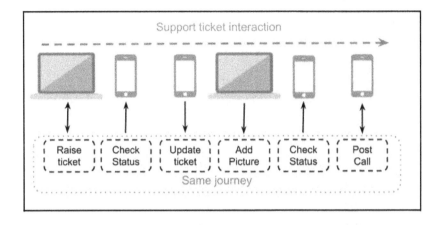

* ★ Test laptop integration as default, with secondary augmentation by mobile
* ★ Consider split journeys that may originate on laptop, but end elsewhere
* ★ Avoid laptop specific features and functionality

Internet of Things

A section on device types, would not be complete without discussing the internet of things (IoT). The pervasive nature of technology, in both the business and consumer world, has seen a plethora of nano-grade innovations to help with home automation, production lines, healthcare and more. Let us break down the IoT into two distinct blocks first of all. Not all IoT devices are the same–there are varying degrees of capabilities, physical size and performance, that in turn impacts how they can be used and what they can be used for. The simplest way to do this is by classifying devices as being *smart* or *constrained.*

Constrained

The definition of a constrained IoT device can be taken from several internet standards and referenced by RFC7744 as being a device "with limited processing power, storage space, and transmission capacities. These devices are often battery-powered and in many cases do not provide user interfaces"[83] The lack of a user interface is significant, as the ability to provide human binding and interaction instantly becomes more complex and potentially limited. Whilst constrained devices may originally have focused on the "unseen" industrial landscape–think production line sensors or programmable logic controllers[84] (PLCs) –constrained devices are now appearing in the consumer world. Examples could include healthcare devices such as network connected pacemakers[85] or diabetes monitors[86].

Smart

At the opposite end of the spectrum, we can classify "smart" devices as essentially being like mini computers. They have capable processors and memory configurations, are able to process encrypted communication links and provide a user interface–if somewhat limited in nature. A simple consumer example, could be the introduction of smart televisions–where the television is essentially able to host installable applications that communicate over TCP/IP

83https://www.rfc-editor.org/rfc/pdfrfc/rfc7744.txt.pdf
84https://en.wikipedia.org/wiki/Programmable_logic_controller
85https://www.theatlantic.com/technology/archive/2018/01/my-pacemaker-is-tracking-me-from-inside-my-body/551681/
86https://www.diabetes.org.uk/guide-to-diabetes/managing-your-diabetes/testing/continuous-glucose-monitoring-cgm

instead of the traditional analog signal. The rise of the personalised television experience driven by individual viewer profiles (see Netflix[87], Amazon [88]or BBC iPlayer[89]), has seen a need to be able to "pair" a physical object with a real identity, that is essentially acting on behalf of the viewer to deliver the viewing experience.

Other examples in the smart object space, could include sports goods[90] and apparel, where professional teams and competent amateurs leverage clothing, balls and equipment to provide technical and timing related metadata. This data can then be used for performance improvement or personalised coaching. Again, the object needs pairing to the individual in order to capture and aggregate signals that can be used for cloud based analytics and insights.

★ Understand that IoT devices have a broad spectrum of capabilities
★ Cater for smart devices, with an eye on constrained
★ Understand how device to identity pairing can provide opportunities for personalisation

The How

Let us take a look at some examples of how multi-device journeys could be implemented.

87 https://help.netflix.com/en/node/10421
88 https://www.amazon.co.uk/gp/help/customer/display.html?ie=UTF8&nodeId=GEM24ZP4GX39MKU4
89 https://www.bbc.co.uk/iplayer/help/questions/signing-in/tv-multiple-accounts
90 https://www.businesswire.com/news/home/20190422005212/en/Global-Smart-Sports-Equipment-Market-2019-2023-Increasing

The first area to consider is that of standardization. By developing standardization at the back end service layer, we can aim to reduce the number of interfaces and APIs that need maintaining. If each device type that is introduced, requires their own distinct interfaces and APIs, suddenly the support and operations cost increases, but also the cross-device experience is unlikely to be seamless or consistent.

Figure 3.8 Standards wrapper for generic device access

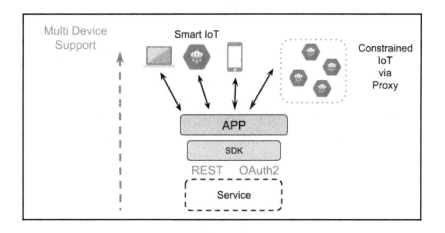

By exposing services via standard interfaces, the level of adoption can increase. A popular design pattern for APIs is to use REST and JSON based payloads. REST[91] (representational state transfer) is an architecture style that

91 https://en.wikipedia.org/wiki/Representational_state_transfer

allows web services to be built around verbs–for example standard HTTP verbs such as GET, PUT or DELETE. Those verbs are then used against a URI (universal resource indicator)–essentially a web address that corresponds to a single resource identifier or group of objects. For example a GET against a URI such as https://myapp.example.com/cars/make/model/1–would return the specific make and model of car with the Id equal to 1. A DELETE against that same URI would remove that car from the underlying data repository.

JSON (javascript object notation)[92] is a data interchange format, that provides a human readable way of transporting and storing data objects. In the above example of calling a GET on the cars repository, the response from the API could be JSON formatted–an object such as the following describing the returned car:

```
{
      "Make" : "Ford",
      "Model" : "Mustang",
      "Id" : "1",
      "Price" : "$45,000",
      "Mileage" : "43302",
      "Color" : "Blue"
}
```

JSON is quite a rich object format, with values being multivalued or indeed further objects. The powerful aspect being there are multiple libraries available for different languages, allowing for the movement of data from an API

92 https://en.wikipedia.org/wiki/JSON

written in say Java, to a consuming application sitting on an IoT device that is written in Go—but both easily able to read and write the standard data format.

Another term that exists in *figure 3.8* is that of OAuth2. OAuth2[93] refers to a IETF (internet engineering task force) standard for open authorization. This won't be the last time we discuss OAuth2 and we'll revisit standards in more detail in *chapter 7.* OAuth2 essentially allows for the sharing of data between multiple different parties, in a standards based way. Again, by being a standard allows for different source and originator systems—perhaps written in different languages and by different teams—the ability to work in an interoperable manner.

SDKs

Whilst standards are a clear way to increase interoperability and reduce operational support complexity, their further adoption can be accelerated by the use of SDKs. Software development kits essentially wrap away the complexity of the first principle APIs. The SDK provides more abstraction and allows applications to be built in a simpler and more repeatable way. The SDK essentially understands two things—the abstracted custom service—so the APIs and expected request and response objects— as well as things specific to the language and device the SDK is written for. So an SDK for a smart IoT device will understand how to interact with the underlying service, in a way the device can tolerate and consume. A different SDK—different in language, but similar in

93https://tools.ietf.org/html/rfc6749

principle—would perform the same function for a laptop consuming information from a JavaScript enabled webpage. The SDKs are then wrapped around specific integration packages for the different different device types.

Figure 3.9 SDK enablement examples

Device Type	Package	SDK function
Laptop	Internet browser	JavaScript library to render JSON response from API in webpage
Smart device	Application written in Go on Linux esque operating system	Go package that wraps OAuth2 authorization calls to allow device pairing to identity
Mobile	Android APK application	Android library that tests for jailbreak status on mobile and sends to cloud REST API during login

★ Look to move towards standardized libraries, interfaces and application exposure points
★ Move away from proprietary or operating specific

modes for authentication and authorization
* Leverage SDKs to accelerate adoption and interoperability

This sector touched on some of the key points around multi-platform journeys and how different devices will be used at different times–but likely within the same user driven event. The powerful use of standards and SDKs not only provides immediate reductions in operational and support complexity, it can also provide a strong foundation for innovation. New device types, user flows and journeys will occur which can be easily catered for with a strong and extendable base.

It is better to spend time expecting change and responding, than being tied to specific technologies and attempting to predict future outcomes.

Let us now take a look at some of the security related requirements of differing device types and journeys and across CIAM in general.

Applying the CIA Triad

What is the CIA triad?

Let us start with the CIA triad–not to be confused with the Central Intelligence Agency–but instead focuses upon the *confidentiality*, *integrity* and *availability* aspects of an information system.

Confidentiality

As the name suggests, confidentiality is an aspect of information security where we're focused on protecting the contents of a payload, message or piece of data from prying eyes, or to quote the ISO27000 standard, making sure "...information is not made available or disclosed to unauthorized individuals, entities or processes".[94]. Clearly in a CIAM landscape, confidentiality becomes very important, as the data involved in that ecosystem is likely to be person related, containing either PII or system usage and activity data, which can be used to infer numerous orthogonal conclusions about someone, if analysed directly, or overlaid with other data.

Integrity

Integrity is really referring to the "accuracy and completeness"[95] of a piece of data. If a piece of data cannot be protected from unwarranted change, it can lose a level of assurance. Sources of truth are seemingly becoming more difficult to come by, in a data driven digital economy, where even the news is now infiltrated by "fake" elements, rendering some of it useless. The integrity aspect of an information security architecture should really focus on two

[94] https://standards.iso.org/ittf/PubliclyAvailableStandards/
[95] https://standards.iso.org/ittf/PubliclyAvailableStandards/

things—one, being able to protect changes to data from unauthorized sources and two, being able to detect unauthorized changes if they do actually occur.

Availability

Availability is really a foundation of any information security project. If a system or service is not available when needed, the rest of the functionality and security controls become less relevant. The aspect of availability is really making sure the right people can access the service at the right time. A secondary part of availability is often tied to resilience—knowing that a system may come under a denial of service attack, but then being in a position where recovery is faster than the attack.

So how does the CIA triad apply specifically to the CIAM landscape? The immediate thought is that it shouldn't—the modern enterprise should be well equipped to handle data breaches, external attacks, insider threats and more. The unfortunate story, is many are not and the foray into providing digital consumer services, is likely to open up new and potentially unknown attack vectors as well being a magnet to new and previously unseen attacks and attackers.

As soon as any system moves beyond userid and passwords as the only user data being stored, an invisible "attack me" sign can appear directly next to the login button. Why?

Well data is valuable. Data relating to user accounts is more valuable. Data relating to actual real identities and people? Gold dust. Attackers can leverage person related data in a myriad of ways, from enhancing synthetic identities to make them look legitimate, to full on impersonation.

Be Secure or Feel Secure?

The paradox of security however—which we touched on briefly in the conflict section in chapter 1—is that an increased security posture can often result in poor user experience. So many digital experiences strive for "frictionless" login, "one-click" signup, "seamless journeys" and so on. However, many end users expect a digital experience to mimic their physical familiarities. If I went to my local bank branch and attempted to withdraw £25,000, I would expect some basic checks—probably show a form of identification, perhaps a fingerprint is taken, maybe I am ushered into a private room (that likely has CCTV) before my hard earned cash is given to me in a crisp envelope.

Those barriers may seem overkill to some who regularly take those sums out, but to many, they would actually instill a level of trust. I would have faith that my bank is performing the necessary checks for money laundering. I would trust that if a fraudster attempted to take *my* money out of *my* account, they would be caught, as the checks would be there to protect *me*. What happens in the digital world? An end user expects similar levels of security—even if the equivalent barriers do not exist. If the experience is too *seamless,* and the inevitable data breach does occur, the immediate thought of the end user would be something along the lines of "can you be surprised, they never check anyway".

The inevitable "speed bump" or "security theatre"[96] however, can help to portray a level of security, which does not actually exist–but can create a *feeling* of security and in turn trust for the end user with the service provider.

Figure 3.10 CIA triad–theatre -v- actual

Security Feature Example	Actual Digital Control	Theatre Overlay
Confidentiality– making sure no malicious third party can listen in on my medical app query	Transparent TLS connection; application authentication via certificates; behaviour analysis	Interruptions for consent; "padlock" notifications; session timeout popups
Integrity– preventing changes to consent decisions for third party app access	Consent receipts that are cryptographically signed; securely persisted on disk	Regular notifications for owner revalidation
Availability– reducing bot	CAPTCHA systems to	Notifications during login

96https://www.schneier.com/blog/archives/2009/11/beyond_security.html

activity that impacts speed and response of login services	automate bot detection; user behaviour analytics	and high volume events

- ★ Analyse security requirements in the context of overall system delivery
- ★ End user trust and "feel" should be considered during implementation
- ★ Security design should occur early and not driven by after implementation audit

Like a physical interaction, notifications and feeling informed, help create trust and understanding. This is even more relevant during a journey that is often unusual to the end user or perhaps only occurs at irregular times, like a house move or mortgage application. Trust is essentially created during small steps, not necessarily by "large gestures", so each part of the journey needs breaking down into smaller composite events.

The CIA triad can then be applied against those smaller events, following standard risk management principles.

Adding in Usability

Let us revisit usability again, by looking at how the priorities towards risk influence implementation practises towards the CIA triad.

The priority assigned to each of the components of the CIA triad will vary, based on the security requirements of the particular project. Those security requirements will be driven by the business appetite to risk–and whether a risk management outcome focuses upon risk mitigation, risk acceptance or risk transfer.

In some scenarios data integrity may trump data availability, where in others, system availability trumps data confidentiality. A few simple examples may solidify the analysis behind this.

Figure 3.11 CIA triad priority examples

Priority: C=confidentiality, I = integrity, A=availability	Example	Reasoning
A > C > I	Production line automation system requires 24x7x365 up time	Capturing, seeing and altering sensor data pertaining to the production line is of lower importance versus cost impact of outage
C > I > A	Secrecy between two parties	Whilst integrity is important, it

	having a telephone call	is likely achievable in addition to secrecy, but not the other way around.
I > C > A	Medical test results	Receiving tamper proof results from a certified source likely trumps their confidentiality, if authenticity cannot be verified

Figure 3.11 really shows three extreme examples—from different industrial sectors, with differing risk appetites—but the aim was to showcase how priorities will shift between confidentiality, integrity and availability even within the small universe of security design and engineering.

If we return now, back to usability, and start to consider usability alongside the framework of the CIA triad—or indeed, even as an extension to—we can start to see how security could be altered with regards to CIAM design concepts.

In *chapter 2*, we visited the conflict between usability and security, and the middle ground of a blended experience is where many organisations try to end up. That middle ground is seeking to normalise the conflict between not only the CIA components in *figure 3.11* but also the "theatre -v- control" overlay from *figure 3.10.*

Figure 3.12 CIA triad + Usability priority examples

Priority: U = Usability, C=confidentiality, I = integrity, A=availability	Example	Reasoning
U + A > C + I	Account registration for a competition implemented during a sports commercial	Peak time commercial creating an urgency factor regarding user participation–forces simplicity for bulk coverage and availability to cover demand spikes
U + A == C + I	Application processing to switch mortgage	Being able to process this entirely online is relatively novel, so simple steps are needed. Due to the financial details involved,

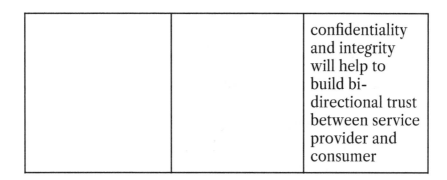

		confidentiality and integrity will help to build bi-directional trust between service provider and consumer

Figure 3.12 attempts to synthesise some scenarios where usability demands could start to alter the traditional CIA hierarchy. Clearly a scenario where U + A < C + I is the typical higher security posture.

Consent Management

Let us change gears again, and take a look at a major requirement when building systems holding consumer related data–that of consent. Consent plays a major role in user interactions and is a key component in both the building of trust and regulatory compliance.

Consent plays a significant part in many different end user interactions–from how and what data can be collected and used, through to the sharing of that data within individuals and third party systems.

Privacy -v- Personalisation

Consent sits within the seemingly paradoxical world of privacy and personalisation. When individuals are asked direct simple questions such as "do you value your privacy" or "do you want your data being kept private", the answer is invariably "YES!". However, not all of our actions are consistent with that behaviour.

Privacy is typically focused on the controlled confidentiality of personally identifiable information (PII). Secrecy on the other hand, is typically associated with computerized functions, such the keeping of cryptographic keys away from prying eyes. The definitions are not necessarily strict, but the subtlety is important, as I think it also generates some of the reasons surrounding behavioural mismatches when it comes to privacy.

Privacy is deemed to be more important to us, as it clearly pertains to something that is an extension of us–PII. Information that can be used maliciously against us, or certainly could be used in ways which we may not authorize or encourage. By association we as human entities place high importance on privacy, in the immediacy. However, we typically view future happiness, with less utility as immediate happiness. $10 in your hand right now, seems more appealing than $12 in a week's time.

The same can essentially be applied to privacy–if a barrier to an immediate service, good or experience exists, due to requirements surrounding privacy preservation or consent capture, the vast majority of people are unlikely to consume the service.

Think of some simple examples.

* Do you pause to read all the terms and conditions when signing up to your favourite online movie store?
* Do you have several different email addresses for all the different online systems you register for?
* Do you distribute buying habits across stores in order to avoid being profiled?

The answer is very likely to be "no" to any or all of the above, resulting in a conflict–similar to that of security versus usability we touched upon in chapter 2.

How can a consumer of a service, receive what they want when they want it via a personalised experience, whilst simultaneously being held in a privacy preserved ecosystem?

There has to be a balanced exchange, between the end user and the service provider–a "coincidence of wants", where both parties perform an exchange in which both parties can be happy. This is an interesting paradox, especially when no money exchanges hands.

The classic problem, of if something is free, you are the product–meaning our data is essentially what the service provider wants, and often needs, in order to deliver a personalised experience.

As a result we end up in conflict and essentially identify another market failure. There is no incentive for the service provider to uphold your privacy, if that privacy inhibits them from delivering a service, which in turn is how they can generate revenue.

Enter stage left, government regulation.

Regulation

As we know regulatory involvement typically occurs during market failure. A simple example of where perhaps we see a monopolistic supplier of a good or service, which requires an external regulator to provide quasi competitive pressure and oversight. It seems when it comes to privacy, we perhaps have another market failure, with the relatively recent introduction to two big pieces of privacy preserving regulation: The EU's GDPR and the California state's CCPA.

GDPR

The GDPR[97] came into effect in May 2018 with essentially two main focus areas:

★ For people to have more control over their data
★ For business to have a level playing field for competition

From a consumer perspective, it was about providing a framework where the processing of an individual's personal data was driven by *consent*, with that consent based on an *affirmative* and *informed* decision. That essentially translates to the end user being made fully

[97]https://ec.europa.eu/info/law/law-topic/data-protection/eu-data-protection-rules_en

aware of what information is being processed, why it is being processed and for the service provider to interrupt the end user to receive a definite positive answer. Typically in the past, a service provider may have received a more implicit answer, based on the user *not* opting out of a particular condition or signup process. The GDPR removes this ambiguity and forces the service provider to be very explicit regarding information capture and use and provide a solid opportunity for opt in and opt out.

GDPR amplifies the data rights of the end user to the following[98]:

★ Data protection by default
★ Data processing information provided to the end user
★ The right to object for the end user
★ Ability to access all the data being kept about the end user
★ Right to be informed if that data is leaked
★ The right to be forgotten

The intervention of any regulation tends to not occur, if the rights are being upheld "naturally" in the evolving digital landscape. Clearly some organisations would have been supporting those rights by default before the GDPR became binding, but many would not.

So what impact does this have on service providers? There are some basic key principles information designers need

98https://ec.europa.eu/info/sites/info/files/virtual_idenitity_en.pdf

to consider when developing digital systems:

- ★ Have clearly defined policies for collecting user data
- ★ Don't use the data for any other reason other than that specified
- ★ Don't collect more data than is needed

In turn that extrapolates into deeper requirements for business[99] such as the following:

1. Check the personal data you collect and process
2. Inform the end user (customer, client, employee) when personal data is collected
3. Keep the personal data for only as long as necessary
4. Secure the data that is being processed
5. Keep and maintain documentation on the data processing activities
6. Make sure the necessary sub contractors abide by the same rules

The above only apply if your business is processing personal data of individuals that reside in the EU—even if the processing entity does not. Clearly if the business resides in the EU too the regulation applies by default.

Many organisations may need to perform a Data Protection Impact Assessment (DPIA) which is a mandatory requirement for organisations that use large amounts of automation, new technologies or there is a higher risk to the end user's freedom. The DPIA process is there to

99https://ec.europa.eu/info/sites/info/files/ds-02-18-544-en-n.pdf

protect the freedoms of the individual if data such as CCTV or facial recognition technology is being used.

Whilst the service provider seems to have onerous new responsibilities, the EU promotes this as a business opportunity–a normalised set of controls that apply to all EU member countries, allowing a service to offer a compliant experience across lots of different countries at once.

CCPA

The CCPA[100] was also introduced in 2018, primarily focused on the state of California in the United States, with an aim of introducing new privacy rights including:

★ The right to know about the personal information a business collects about them and how it is used and shared
★ The right to delete personal information collected from them
★ The right to opt-out of the sale of their personal information; and
★ The right to non-discrimination for exercising their CCPA rights

A Californian resident may now ask a business to disclose what personal information they hold about the end user, what they do with it, who they share it with and request that it can be deleted. There is also a right for the business

100https://oag.ca.gov/privacy/ccpa

to notify the end user when data is being collected.

The personal data definition under the CCPA, is typically data that is not publicly available, including things like purchase history, browsing history and preferences.

The CCPA needs to be upheld by organisations (other than non-profits or government agencies) either earning more than $25 million per year, holds data on over 50,000 Californian residents or services more than 50% of their revenue from selling data on Californian residents.

Whilst both the GDPR and CCPA are now law, the actual number of organisations being fully compliant is still unknown. The impact of not doing for service providers however can be substantial, with non-compliance for GDPR potentially resulting in a maximum 20 million Euro fine (or 4% annual turnover whichever is the larger)[101]. From a CCPA perspective, individuals can only take legal action against a provider in the event of a data breach, that also shows that customer data was not adequately protected–aka was not encrypted or redacted. A statutory damages limit is set at $750 per incident.

Not withholding the monetary impact, the brand damage and potential share price impact of a public non-compliance charge, must also be taken into account.

Consent Lifecycle

So now we are in a digital ecosystem, where many regions

101https://www.itgovernance.co.uk/dpa-and-gdpr-penalties

and services will be impacted by some examples of privacy preservation regulation. Let us briefly break down, how consent can contribute to that process and the different states of an example consent lifecycle.

Capture

> The first step is the ability to capture a consent opinion. That event is likely to be triggered by circumstances described within one of the appropriate regulatory controls—so during the initial capture of a piece of personal information. The consent question, if you will, needs to be well described, using non-legalese language, that allows the end user to be fully informed, regarding why the information is needed and for what purpose it will be used. It is quite common for each piece of personal data being captured, to have its own micro-terms and explanation—instead of the traditional macro scale terms and conditions that covers an entire relationship between the end user and service provider. The consent capture process would likely need to be affirmative too—so essentially the user actively opting in, instead of passively having to opt out.

Store

> So the capture process needs to clearly support things like non-repudiation and a base level of security—to allow for the consent decision to be

authenticated and not changed after the fact. The capture object, often referred to a receipt, is likely to contain various pieces of meta information, such as the identifier of the user, the attributes and events being consented to, the consent decision, and any necessary timestamping data too. An example of a receipt schema is seen by the Kantara Initiative's Consent Receipt project[102]. The consent receipt then needs storing, likely alongside a user profile record, or linkable in a separate store. That store requires tamper proofing–with the necessary protection and detection controls in place.

Revoke

But what use is a consent process, if the end user cannot revoke a previously granted consent event? This generates two questions–can the user easily revoke? What process needs fulfilling to allow the revocation to complete? The first will require a user interface where an end user can make self-service requests, that are simple to operate and again are affirmative. A central control panel is likely, where a simple single dashboard is available, that shows what personal data is held, where it is being used, the reason for it being held and the consequences of a revoke action. The consequences are likely to be simple explanations that certain features will no longer work, be less personalised or feature rich. A revocation event triggered by an end user action,

102https://kantarainitiative.org/download/7902/

then needs upholding and fulfilling. What applications need notifying? What information needs removing, or no longer accessible for future requests? What do the downstream applications need to do in order to fulfil the revocation event? And how do they communicate that process has completed back to the central consent store? Questions like these need to be considered when designing the personal data workflows.

Audit

One final piece to mention, is the audit process. All of the events mentioned above, clearly need to be documented in a replayable, time stamp driven audit history. That audit process needs to capture (also in a privacy preserving way) the various different actions that have taken place, by whom, when and why. It is likely that the audit process could be used to fulfil any necessary compliance requirements, so again needs the same levels of tamper proofing and storage for any sensitive set of transactions.

Privacy as a Differentiator

Let us end this section on consent, by taking a business look at the impact of privacy preservation to the service provider, in the context of competitive differentiation.

Whilst it seems clear, that privacy could in fact be a market failure, where the service provider sees no immediate benefit in upholding many different aspects of preservation–especially if that comes into conflict with existing business models–is there a place for a business to see privacy as a competitive difference–something that can build trust with end users?

Let us take a brief look at the software and hardware giant Apple. Their UK privacy policy[103] at the time of writing states:

"Privacy is a fundamental human right. At Apple, it's also one of our core values. Your devices are important to so many parts of your life. What you share from those experiences, and whom you share it with, should be up to you. We design Apple products to protect your privacy and give you control over your information. It's not always easy. But that's the kind of innovation we believe in."

That is a pretty powerful statement. Describing privacy as a fundamental right passes the pressure to its competitors–stating basically, that privacy should be a given in every transaction, device and event–with an assumptive close, that everyone should be doing this anyway.

Having privacy as a core value seems to suggest they have left-shifted the principle to be present within every design, build and implementation phase of the products and services they create. They also acknowledge that privacy is not easy–opening up the fact they are likely to get things

103https://www.apple.com/uk/privacy/

wrong in the future.

Is that level of transparency covering their reputation, or does it have a marked way in improving end user trust in them as an organization and service provider?

Trust is typically built within the physical human to human world, by lots of smaller interactions and steps, rather than the single grand gesture. How does that trust building process translate into the digital landscape? The organisational privacy policy is likely to be the equivalent of the grand gesture—something to look towards in times of trouble—whilst the actual trust building element is likely to be driven by the small, often minute aspects of signup, settings, revocation, notifications, integration transparency and potential data breach activity handling.

Organisations like Apple have a highly inelastic level of demand and support from their consumer base—you are either an Apple fan-boi (or girl) or not. The same can be said for other competing giants such as Google or Samsung. Competition tends to be oligopic in nature and not based on price, but instead on branding and perceived value. Privacy is certainly a characteristic that is likely to be assessed in that area of perceived value. The likelihood is that once trust is lost—due to privacy erosion or not—it is likely to spread extremely quickly to vast swathes of an inelastic user population—as the user community is likely to hold very similar values. If those values are diminished it can be very hard to rectify. Using privacy as a differentiator could be a difficult position to perhaps uphold long term.

Summary

In this chapter we touched on some of the relatively new requirements that occur during CIAM deployments. Personalisation, usability and privacy can be complex to implement and more importantly maintain over the lifecycle of an application or service.

Those requirements are also likely to change rapidly due to external factors such as regulation, trends and technological advancement.

All CIAM projects need to put the end user first in their design strategy. No longer is the service enough—it needs to be tailored in such a way that the consumer feels listened to, and is treated with respect, in a simple and transparent way.

Chapter 4 will see us design the CIAM lifecycle—taking us on a journey a service provider is likely to take when implementing the various stages of customer data acquisition and use.

CHAPTER 4

CIAM Lifecycle

This chapter will focus upon the CIAM lifecycle–an example end to end analysis of the key steps a consumer identity will take whilst accessing services, goods and experiences from the service owner.

For each section, we will then dig into some examples of what those stages may look like, investigating some basic design patterns and trends.

Figure 4.1 The CIAM Lifecycle

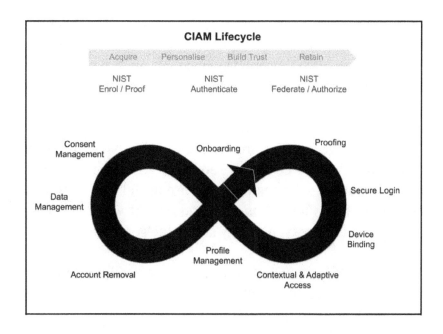

In *figure 4.1* we describe the basic lifecycle as containing 9 distinct stages:

1. Onboarding
2. Proofing
3. Secure Login
4. Device Binding
5. Contextual & Adaptive Access
6. Profile Management
7. Consent Management
8. Data Management
9. Account Removal

A basic linear flow typically occurs, where Onboarding would clearly occur before Profile Management. But some aspects can be more modular or integrated independently. For example Data Management may occur alongside Secure Login and Consent Management, with limited need for Proofing in one particular journey.

Figure 4.1 also contains too other references to help us model the life cycle–a reference to the NIST Identity Guidelines[104] and a customer retention flow, typically used by marketers or sales teams. Both are useful barometers in helping us focus upon being a good citizen when it comes to consumer security, usability and value generation.

The NIST Identity Guidelines are a set of best practice documents issued by the National Standards Institute in the US aimed primarily at federal agencies and departments.

104https://pages.nist.gov/800-63-3/

The standards help define authentication, proofing and federation specifications and promote secure interoperability. The main meat of the content is broken down into three different documents—namely Enrollment & Identity Proofing SP800-63A, Authentication & Lifecycle Management SP800-63B and Federation & Assertions SP800-63C. As we walk through the lifecycle, we can reference back to some examples from those guides in our analysis.

The *Acquire-Personalise-Build Trust-Retain* linkage, is to focus our attention on the entire reason the CIAM lifecycle—and indeed the entire subject area of CIAM actually exists—is that to provide services, applications and experiences to external users in order to grow revenue or build communities. Again we will reference that flow as we discuss each step in the life cycle.

Onboarding

Clearly before any interactions can take place between a user and the underlying service, an onboarding ceremony must occur. The service provider needs to know enough information to at least authenticate the user in future interactions—and typically requires much more in order to deliver personalisation. Let us take a look at some onboarding options.

Bot Detection
Firstly, let's add a brief pre-section on bot detection.

Whilst this process isn't solely related to onboarding—it's typically applied at all parts of the CIAM lifecycle—the first interaction with the user community will be during registration, so let's start with making sure we're detecting fake or automated attempts at creating accounts.

Bots or drones, are simply pieces of software—often classified as malware—whose sole aim is to create fake identities, at scale. Fake accounts have a significant impact. They firstly skew any analytics that the service may need. Secondly they can then be used for fraudulent attacks such as generating fake comments, referrals or recommendations. A high percentage of fake accounts will also have an impact on operational costs—either in the form of per seat licensing, network bandwidth or increased profile storage.

The most simple barrier is to use a CAPTCHA system—which stands for completely automated public Turing test to tell computers and humans apart! A long acronym for a useful tool. The most common is probably Google's reCAPTCHA[105], which allows for simple configuration into a webpage to help identify and block malicious and potentially automated activity. There are other approaches based on network threat analysis too. It's essential that any of the public Internet facing registration, login and credential reset pages have at least basic bot protection.

105https://www.google.com/recaptcha/about/

Anonymous User

Let us start the onboarding process, by looking at anonymous user registrations. But anonymous is not really anonymous. Many service providers provide a certain level of functionality that doesn't require a user to actively onboard to the service. This is often common in low touch, high volume processes, when a user is typically in a position of low commitment. An example of this, is perhaps getting a quote for car insurance or researching a product or service. During this really early stage, there is limited incentive for the user to provide basic identity or contact information in exchange for the service being used. As the transaction being performed is often fast and likely a convenience good, with multiple competing substitution services available, the service provider may want to remove as many barriers to access as possible—and signup could be seen as a barrier.

The service provider however, may want a way to uniquely identify each end user interaction. This could help analytics, reduce fraud or start the process of migrating the user from an unknown to a known entity. There are several common ways of achieving this, using a combination of device and interaction metadata. This metadata essentially helps to create a "fingerprint" of the interaction, which includes capturing device characteristics, such as IP address, operating system version, Internet browser version and configuration. That information is then often put through a hash function, to create a relatively short random looking value.

For example take the following pieces of information and pass through the sha256sum[106] hashing algorithm:

```
IP address: 10.1.8.109
User-Agent: Mozilla/5.0 (X11; Linux x86_64)
AppleWebKit/537.36 (KHTML, like Gecko)
Chrome/85.0.4183.102 Safari/537.36
```

The result is:

c01cfd1a7393c016b11336a91a9a681a8c07b2f51be7eac82e76e6f3f1027fbf.

A pretty long value that doesn't reveal much about the underlying user or device. The service provider however, can use that to start to build a profile of the interaction. The next time the same device on the same IP address visits, a quick comparison to existing hashes can reveal if the interaction is with a new user or someone they have seen before. A rudimentary way to track the interactions.

The User-Agent value is pretty coarse grained (and spoofable) and in reality would likely be replaced by a script that runs inside a web page to help capture a detailed profile of the client device. There are numerous open source libraries[107] available on Github that can help to provide accurate finger prints.

★ Anonymous profiling is useful where signup is seen as an unnecessary barrier

106https://manpages.ubuntu.com/manpages/trusty/man1/sha256sum.1.html
107https://github.com/jackspirou/clientjs

* ★ Provide notification and consent options regarding information capture
* ★ Be conscientious with regards privacy preservation when storing or sharing captured information

Manual Entry

The next level in an onboarding flow, would be for the end user to actively present some further information about themselves. We have all been faced with large self service forms, asking for a username, password and sometimes lots of other pieces of information, such as date of birth, sex, postal address and more. Whilst still common, they don't always generate the best possible user experience–they are repetitive, prone to input error and are typically treated with a relatively low level of assurance by the service provider. How can they differentiate one "John Smith" from another?

In some circumstances though, a basic form to collect information, provides a useful exercise–it can help to identify a level of interest and commitment from the end user towards a service.

The information typically captured is likely to be an email address and password–two basic attributes used for a returning user to authenticate themselves. The email address–typically used for notifications and communications if consent has been captured–is the most common form of identifier. It is globally unique, so helps to tie a specific user to the service. Other options include capturing not just an email address, but also giving the end user the ability to choose a specific username for the service. This allows them to create a moniker or nickname that can help provide a basic level of anonymity from other users on the system if interactions such as forums or blog comments are enabled.

★ On initial registration, capture only the information needed to authenticate as a returning user
★ Provide notification and consent options regarding use of email addresses
★ Allow password fields to be accessed and populated by password managers and vaults to allow the submission of complex passwords

BYOI

We all have stories of terrible manual form filling when it comes to signing up to our favourite services. To remove that perceived barrier, BYOI–bring your own identity–comes to the rescue, by at least helping to provide a more seamless experience.

The concept here is that the service provider allows the end user to provide identity and profile information that is essentially already stored somewhere else. That somewhere else is typically referred to as an "identity provider". The most common ones are the big social media players such as Facebook, LinkedIn, Twitter or Google.

The assumption is that the user you want to register for your service, has already registered a profile elsewhere—and you can piggyback onto that process and harvest the information the user has already provided.

Figure 4.2 Simplified BYOI flow

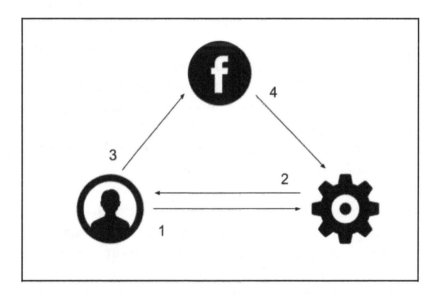

This process generates a few new concepts to think about. Firstly how does your service contact the identity provider and make the necessary request to harvest attributes? A standard way of achieving this is using the OAuth2[108] protocol. We will cover OAuth2 in greater detail in *chapter 7.* For now, we just need to acknowledge there is a standards based way for a service provider (or relying party in OAuth2 parlance) to request attributes and data from the identity provider. It is up to the identity provider, to then

108https://tools.ietf.org/html/rfc6749

provide the end user with all the necessary notifications and consent management options, regarding sending their identity data to the new service provider

So why is this approach popular? Well it can help solve a few barriers to the registration process. Firstly, the end user doesn't need to repeatedly provide different service providers with similar information. The second one is slightly more subtle and is related to password storage. The flow in *figure 4.2* can also be used for subsequent login journeys. Instead of providing a username and password to the service on future logins, the service provider essentially uses a token issued by the social provider to authenticate the user locally. We will discuss the pros and cons of this approach in the Secure Login section.

Other examples of BYOI need not focus just on social providers. Other potentially more trusted sources of identity data could come from government sources, or providers related to housing identity data for national services. In the UK for example project Verify[109] provides a framework for quasi private sector organisations such as the Post Office and various banking organisations to act as identity providers to government services.

A final comment on distributed identities—often referred to as self sovereign identities[110]. These types of identities often utilise technology based on block chain[111], providing

109https://www.gov.uk/government/publications/introducing-govuk-verify/introducing-govuk-verify
110https://medium.com/metadium/introduction-to-self-sovereign-identity-and-its-10-guiding-principles-97c1ba603872
111https://www.computerworld.com/article/3191077/what-is-blockchain-the-

anonymous, cryptographically secure means of sharing identity related attributes to those you trust and those you don't. When developing a service that requires identity data, integration into this space is a worthwhile research exercise.

★ One-click signup reduces friction—especially on mobile devices
★ Consider capturing changes on the social provider during subsequent access to the service
★ Can the identity provider be trusted—what level of assurance should be placed on the data that is harvested?
★ Consider augmenting identity data from the third party provider with information captured elsewhere, that has a different assurance level

Migration

A third area to consider with regards to user onboarding is that of user migration—getting users into a system from an existing project or deployment. A simple answer is to replicate, copy or bulk upload data from one source repository into the new service user database or directory. There are multiple open source and proprietary systems for migrating data from say a SQL or noSQL database to an LDAP directory and vice versa, with a focus on continual replication of data until one system becomes authoritative. Another option is a one off bulk upload process—exposing an API that can consume a human readable CSV or JSON

complete-guide.html

formatted file containing the user data.

It is common however, that with any data migration process, a cleanup of the data also takes place, in order to remove redundant, duplicate or inactive accounts. A few ways are often leveraged to accomplish this. Firstly, set a threshold regarding previous user activity–if an account has not been logged into for x-months, migrate, but disable within the target repository. During a grace or account recovery phase, the disabled account could be re-activated via some sort of out of band process–perhaps via a help desk call, revalidation process or other. Set a secondary threshold on this grace period window, before finally removing the account entirely–or moving to archive–in order to leave only active users in the new repository.

A slightly different approach is to only migrate accounts for those who are actively logging into the new service. This requires the new service to have access to the existing user repository to validate login credentials. Once the validation has taken place the user is migrated. Any users not logging in are simply left behind in the old repository.

- ★ Data replication, synchronization and transformation services are common for CSV, JSON, LDAP, SQL and noSQL
- ★ Consider data cleansing automation during data migration
- ★ Identify active users and provide workflows for disabling and archiving

Account Validation

So we now have several potential methods of getting some initial user data into the new service repository. Next, we need to consider account validation options. This is a basic step to apply some freshness and liveness checks to the basic account that has been created. This basic account validation typically focuses on the email address used during the onboarding. A mail is sent to the user's registered address with a link to continue the onboarding process or to "validate" the account. This link is likely to be time sensitive and not to be used by other email addresses. The idea behind this, is to first validate the commitment of the user entering the data into the form or otherwise and second, to actually make sure the email address used during registration is owned and accessible by the same person who entered it.

Whilst a basic check, it can stop the start of a synthetic account creation process–where real data is used by a fraudulent actor in order to create the basic account profile.

- ★ Tag user accounts with attributes such as "validated" or "email-verified" in order to start the account assurance process
- ★ Use a link tied to a specific email address, with a time out on link lifetime
- ★ The validation process can also be used to capture active consent of the sign up process and to acknowledge ownership of the email address given

Account validation is a basic level of proofing–where you start to build a level of assurance associated with individual attributes that have been collected and what level of trust you can place in them. We can now move onto more complex identity proofing concepts.

So far in the CIAM lifecycle, we have looked at the most basic step in the process–getting people to register for service. In the sales funnel, this "acquire" process is crucial in building a community or revenue. That initial onboarding needs to promote inclusion, membership and partnership and remove as many barriers or decisions the user has to make as possible. We need to think seamless and secure. The user does not want to have to make decisions during that process. The more decisions, clicks or steps they have to make, they less likely they will complete the process.

Proofing

In some cases a service provider may not care about the entity they are interacting with–perhaps in cases where anonymity (or pseudonymity) is required by the end user and is actually seen as a prerequisite for using a service. Clearly in other circumstances, there will be a requirement to obtain a higher level of assurance with regards to the person the service is interacting with–think health care interactions or financial transactions. In such circumstances, the identity attributes being used need to be validated and verified.

NIST 800-63A[112] is specifically focused upon providing guidance for enrolment and proofing services. The document prescribes three distinct identity assurance levels (IALs):

- IAL1: the identity attributes are essentially self asserted and provide no guarantee of linkage to a real life person
- IAL2: evidence exists that the claimed identity is associated with a real life person, with a need for physically present verification
- IAL3: physical presence is required for identity and authorized by a trained representative

The processing flow typically takes in three steps: Resolution, Validation and Verification as shown in *figure 4.3*.

Figure 4.3 NIST 800-63A proofing flow

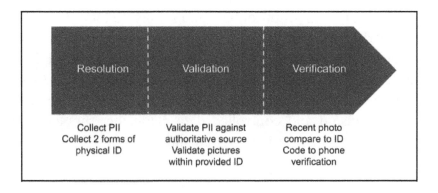

Each service will have their own requirements regarding

112https://nvlpubs.nist.gov/nistpubs/SpecialPublications/NIST.SP.800-63a.pdf

identity attribute proofing and clearly some may not need physical identity card or passport validation. The process can be time consuming and costly to administer and will likely be limited to organisations within the financial services arena. There are however, dedicated third party proofing services that can be subscribed to and integrated easily into existing registration journeys.

The second area of interest from 800-63A, is that of identity verification. The proofing aspect is really to ascertain that an identity exists. The subtly different second step, is to map the verified identity against the person who claims they are that person—more a digital binding step. There are 5 main levels of verification: Unacceptable, Weak, Fair, Strong and Superior. A "Superior" rating, would leverage biometric capture and comparison. A "Fair" verification is likely the most common, which would focus upon testing knowledge or perhaps performing a remote physical comparison.

A "cheaper" form of proofing could simply be focused upon comparison of trusted data sources to those that are self asserted. For example the mapping of financial transaction data, such as the last 3 transactions on a credit card. One source of data for these sorts of comparisons must come from a trusted and controlled data plane that the service provider has previously validated and verified.

Secure Login

At some point your user community will log in, or

authenticate. The most basic process is the typical username and password combination we are all familiar with. We will touch on password management a little later in the life cycle, but the theme that has emerged in recent years, is that password based authentication provides a relatively low level of security.

There are two threads to consider when understanding password based security. Firstly the impact of the end user. Essentially the user's behaviour is out of the scope of control of the service provider. Each user will behave differently and will not always make the most consistent or secure choices. Their main aim is to access a service, not care about security.

User threats to password based login include:

★ Poor choice of password, that is easy to crack
★ A password used on other systems
★ A password similar to one used on other systems–often incremented by a number
★ Complex passwords are hard to remember are often written down

From a service provider perspective, they also have a responsibility with regards password based authentication. They need to focus upon:

★ Selecting a secure way to store a password–hashing over encryption
★ Protecting the repositories where passwords are

stored
★ Devising password policies that solve both usability and security

If passwords are so bad, what are the alternatives? Multi factor authentication (MFA) is clearly an option–where the username and password is used in *combination* with something else. MFA typically focuses upon leveraging two from "something you are", "something you know" and "something you have". Let us look into a few options that could satisfy this requirement.

MFA

Let us break down the various options into their subsequent category and perform a basic analysis on the implementation costs and benefits.

Figure 4.4 Something you are authentication options

Option	Cost	Benefit	Comments
Biometric–Voice	Moderate	Useful for telephone based transactions, call centre pre-authentication and handling.	Analyses signatures of how words are sounded which is stored against the user profile.
Biometric–	Low to	Leverages	Iris sits at the

Iris	Moderate	camera technology so can potentially be a scalable option.	front of the eye and manages inbound light. Not as accurate as a retina scan.
Biometric– Retina	High	Retina changes little over a person's lifetime, so good for long term use. High degree of user uniqueness–even twins have different values.	Retina is part of the back of the eye. The unique signature is based on the retinal capillaries. Military uses. Requires specialist technology.
Biometric– Fingerprint	Low to Moderate	Becoming stable within standard iOS/Android phones, making it both scalable and accessible to large user populations.	Either optical or electrocurrent methods are used to measure friction ridges and minutiae on the fingertip. May exclude some parts of the user

			population.
Biometric–Face Picture	Low to Moderate	Contactless and non-evasive. Amplified in popularity by Apple's faceID–meaning user education is high.	Camera based process of mapping face topology to known existing pictures. CCTV based Human-Identification-at-a-Distance (HID) requires specialist pictorial enhancing techniques.
Behaviour–Typing Pattern	Low to Moderate	Relatively non-invasive, especially for users logging in from a laptop. Less useful for mobile-first deployments.	Also known as keystroke dynamics–it focuses upon typing speeds and gaps between letters to create a per user signature.

Behaviour–Device Handling	Low to Moderate	Relatively non-invasive for mobile phone users. Typically used in conjunction with a PIN.	Focuses on things like gait, phone angle, touch sensitivity and other factors relating to physical device usage.

Something you are MFA options, are the ones often seen in the sci-fi movies–opening space shuttle doors via an eye scanner or launching the nuclear missile with a fingerprint. Whilst the future may well be here today in some respects, the selection of a biometric based authentication or MFA option, is likely to take into account a few different pieces of analysis.

Whatever biometric is chosen, is likely to have a level of accuracy associated with it–often resulting in false positives (letting the bad guys in when you shouldn't and often known as the false acceptance rate) and false negatives (stopping the good guys getting in when you should, often known as the false rejection rate). The ideal union of each of those measurements is called the "crossover" rate. This essentially provides a balance between the two outcomes.

When looking at biometric adoption, it is also worth focusing on simple operational factors, such as user enrolment to the service, user signature change or rotation as well as less technical aspects, such as education and understanding by the user community. If no one wants to enrol to the biometric, the security benefits diminish spectacularly.

So what other options do we have in the MFA race, if biometrics are not a practical immediate deployment option?

Figure 4.5 Something you know authentication options

Option	Cost	Benefit	Comments
Password	Low	Universally accepted, rightly or wrongly as the defacto authenticatio n option. Most MFA journeys start with password by default.	Effectively "free" in most systems due to strong library and configuration support. Strong attack focus due to poor quality or storage choices.
Partial Password	Low	Often seen in the financial services sector, with focus on usability.	Arguably less secure than password, depending on how the individual characters are stored. Potentially

			slower to process.
PIN	Low	Common on mobile phones as default unlock. Users are relatively well educated in picking non-default values.	Low security if used on their own, with a 1 in 10,000 (4 digits) or 1 in a million (6 digits) chance of an attacker guessing correctly the first time. Easily brute forcible and requires strict lockout policies on incorrect entry.
Knowledge Based	Low	Doesn't require the user to remember anything new as knowledge is often relating to their history—meaning uptake is high.	Low security, with vast swathes of personal data available on the Internet to combat the obvious questions such as first school or first job.
Pattern	Low to	Leveraged on	Relatively good

	Moderate	mobile phones with touch screen capabilities, the user draws a unique pattern on the screen instead of a PIN.	with regards to usability, but relatively low on coverage, due to dependency on modern touch screen phones. Likely replaced by fingerprint/face print.
Passphrase	Low to Moderate	A 5-6 word phrase—often from a movie, book, song and combined with a date.	Higher security than passwords and can improve usability as often user chosen. Slightly increases storage and processing costs with regard to hashing/encryption. Often mandatory for password managers and vaults as password replacement.

The vast majority of the something you know options, are typically used to replace passwords–especially PIN for mobiles and passphrase for vaulting systems. Relying solely on something you know for the second factor, is arguably not a second factor if the classic username and password are chosen as the initial authenticator.

Let us briefly look at some examples from the third category: something you have.

Figure 4.5 Something you have authentication options

Option	Cost	Benefit	Comments
Phone (as a token)	Low	Scalable due to the proliferation of smart phone technology. Strong existing user education and simple enrol/use.	Associated with downloading a pre-built mobile app, that often contains the ability to receive "push" notifications from the provider. The end user responds to the push event with a local authentication step between the user and phone. Proves ownership of the pre-registered

			phone/app combination
OTP SMS	Low	Cheap, simple to implement and easy to use.	A server side generated one time password (OTP) is sent via an SMS text message to the user's pre-registered mobile device. That code is then entered into a web page for comparison. Due to insecurities in public switched telephone networks, NIST recommends[113] this is not a secure long term MFA option.
OTP Email	Low	Cheap, simple to implement and easy to use.	A server side generated one time password (OTP) is sent via an email message to the user's pre-registered email address. That code is then

113https://pages.nist.gov/800-63-FAQ/

			entered into a web page for comparison. Due to insecurities in email technology, like SMS above, NIST recommends this should not be a secure long term MFA option.
OTP App Generated	Low to Moderate	Cryptographic standardized way of generating a one time password that doesn't involve SMS/email communications. Simple to use, and gaining popularity amongst social providers	The end user would use a locally installed application that supports the OATH[114] one time password generation algorithm. Free examples include Google Authenticator[115]. During login the end user and server side components generate the same OTP using a shared secret. During enrolment that

114https://openauthentication.org/
115https://play.google.com/store/apps/details?
id=com.google.android.apps.authenticator2

			shared secret would need adding to the generator–typically by the end user scanning a QR code.
OTP Hardware Generated	Moderate to High	Transactions requiring higher assurance such as banking, may require physical hardware tokens to generate OTPs.	Enrolment and management of hardware fobs increases cost substantially, but also provides a higher level of control and security.
Smart Card	Moderate to High	Mature and reliable technology, used primarily for workforce users who require high levels of assurance.	Smart cards (personal identity verification card in the US) can essentially hold key material and other user meta data. Often used to access physical buildings as well as being read by USB devices plugged into laptops. Unlikely to be used in many standard CIAM deployments

			due to cost and operational support.
Hardware Fob	Moderate to High	High level of tamper proof security. Wide range of commercially available devices with differing integration options, that are relatively cheap ($35).	A portable device, typically attached to a key ring, that integrates to a laptop via USB, or via Bluetooth and NFC to a mobile. Can perform cryptographicall y secure challenge response authentication

Figure 4.4, figure 4.5 and *figure 4.6* provide some basic examples of the types of commercially available MFA options that could be implemented relatively simply in a CIAM environment. Not only do operational costs and usability play a part in determining what to implement, the security aspect plays a huge part too.

NIST 800-63B[116] is focused upon Authentication and associated Lifecycle Management and provides guidance around different authenticator assurance levels (AAL's) regarding how a user authenticates themselves. They can be a useful barometer when deciding if an MFA is needed (they're always needed!) and if so what type. NIST 800-

116https://pages.nist.gov/800-63-3/sp800-63b.html

63B lists the AAL's as follows:

- AAL1–provides *some* assurance that the user controls the authenticator bound to their account. The end user must provide evidence of possession and control of the authenticator, in either a single or multi factor environment

- AA2–provides *high* confidence that the user controls the authenticator bound to their account. Two different authentication factors must be satisfied. AAL2 also requires approved cryptographic techniques

- AAL3–provides *very high* confidence that the user controls the authenticator bound to their account. This includes use of proof of possession of a key via cryptographic means. The two authenticators required are a hardware based authenticator and a verifier impersonation resistant authenticator

If we analyse some of the examples we've touched upon already, a memorized secret and a single factor OTP would classify as AAL1. For AAL2 a memorized secret *and* a secondary factor based on something you have would be sufficient, with the second factor being a crypto based OTP–either in software or hardware. AAL3 really requires the use of a hardware device in conjunction with something like a crypto based OTP generator.

Clearly the requirements for a consumer facing service will

vary substantially, with only the most sensitive events involving financial services or health care transactions likely to require hardware.

With the improved security posture of many social media providers ever increasing, many end users will feel comfortable with concepts such as push authentication, mobile app download and install and entering one time passwords—even if those passwords are being sent in relatively low assurance means such as SMS or email. Those options would seem like table stakes for many projects during an initial release.

★ Focus MFA selection on a blended experience of security and usability
★ Aim for a combination of options that can cover the largest number of user communities
★ Provide choice and abstract integrations to allow a future roadmap to adapt to changes in technological innovations and user trends

Passwordless

Whilst MFA is really a booster to the sticking plaster of password based authentication, we should really take a voyage into the world of passwordless. If we solve the underlying issue with passwords do we need MFA at all?

Well that is still debatable, depending on the single factor that is chosen to replace passwords. Some of the factors described in *figure 4.4, figure 4.5 and figure 4.6* could be used as password replacements–namely a decent cryptographic based OTP. The usability aspect of always having to enter an OTP–instead of the typical scenario of only when something suspicious has been spotted–may grate on the user community however.

Magic Link

A couple of other options could include the use of a "magic" link. A magic link essentially leverages the same approach an OTP delivered via email. The user initiates a process supplying their identifier or email address and the back end service sends a link to a pre-registered email address. On clicking the link, the user is automatically logged in via a web browser. The use of the link is clearly a weak spot and anyone with access to the registered email account can log in. The link must also be single use and tied to some sort of server side verification, which doesn't leak information when used.

WebAuthn

Whilst cryptographic based authentication methods for OTP or challenge response style flows are common using hardware based fobs or tokens, in a CIAM deployment they might only apply to a small percentage of the user community, due to cost and operational impact. Another alternative is a relatively recent addition to standards based authentication which is WebAuthn. A standard promoted by the W3C[117] and promoted by the likes of Microsoft and Yubico, WebAuthn promises to deliver a secure, standards based way to securely authenticate a user over a modern web browser using a cryptographically secure means. We'll cover the details of WebAuthn in *chapter 7*, but the high level concept is the creation of secure keys that can be stored within modern mobile phones or even the Mac OS. Those keys never leave the device and are used to answer a challenge during the login process. The service provider doesn't need to store anything other than publicly available information to allow the user to log in.

Whilst passwordless may well be a panacea for many systems, the practical aspects of deployment in an Internet facing system will be large. Enrolment, reset and usability will play a part, as will education regarding user behaviour. Passwords have become so ubiquitous that a change to login without them, may actually make the end user feel *less secure* when in fact the opposite may be true.

- ★ Consider roadmaps for passwordless based technologies
- ★ Start to introduce passwordless via staggered journeys
- ★ Leverage differing methods of user education to increase adoption and build trust

117https://www.w3.org/TR/webauthn/

SSO

So what is the main premise of logging in? One of them will clearly be access to services, goods and applications. Part of that process however, may well require access to lots of other peer systems. The end user is likely to have no interest in logging in multiple times using the same credentials. This is where SSO, or single sign on, comes into play. Here the user authenticates once, and the resulting cookie or session can be used to access lots of other services—either controlled by the service provider, or perhaps even via a federation relationship with trusted 3rd parties.

SSO services typically rely on a service side database keeping a track of all the issued sessions and cookies. When a user has completed a successful authentication process, a cookie will be set in the user's browser for a particular domain or application URL with associated metadata such as when the cookie will expire. The server will also have a database of associated sessions and their expiry.

Applications within the same domain—for example *app1.example.com* and *app2.example.com*—are relatively easy to set up using the same session objects. In other scenarios a user logged into *app1.example.com* may also need to access something in *app2.different.com*—in which case cross domain single sign on is needed, and may require more sophisticated cookie trust and exchange services.

Mobile device SSO is also a hot topic. The idea of logging in with a username and password on a mobile device will send shivers down the spines of many users—especially if there are complex password requirements in place. Password managers and vaults can help here of course by storing and filling in login forms within mobile applications.

However, SSO across mobile applications from the same service provider should be a key goal to improve usability and reduce operational complexity of having to manage an ever growing list of session objects for each application. Applications from the same provider (and signed and managed by the same developer process) can act together within the mobile operating system to access stored objects and other cookie and session material.

This should certainly be an area of focus, if the service is deploying multiple mobile applications.

A final thought on SSO—there is often a requirement surrounding inbound account linking. In an ecosystem supporting BYOI use cases, it may be common to link multiple different accounts together. For example, signing up and logging in with Facebook on one visit, but then logging in with Google the next. The service provider may need a function to link one inbound social provider to another—likely using an attribute shared between the two providers. Email address is a common attribute to use for obvious reasons. The linking process should also include affirmative steps, actively seeking permission, consent and understanding that accounts are being linked together.

Device Binding

Let us move onto an area that is implicitly linked to the login process–that of device binding. Regardless of how the end user is authenticated to a service, they need to do so from an Internet connected device. Technically it could be argued it's actually the device doing the authenticating and not the entity presenting a set of credentials. For the sake of the analysis, we can focus upon two distinct flows–the user identity authentication and potentially that of the device too–either in parallel or sequentially.

In a workforce environment, the identity and access management controls can be applied not only to people and processes, but also to systems and devices too, as everything within the organisational "world" can be under management. Devices can be assigned to employees, devices can have standard builds and configurations and numerous other security controls can be put in place.

In the CIAM world, a lot of control is lost. End user communities have different patterns of usage, behaviour, signup trends and more. The devices they use are not controlled by the service provider. In the case of promoting the installation of a service provider mobile app, each mobile device may well be a different model, be running different operating system versions and have different applications already installed–all with differing levels of associated assurance.

How can the service provider start to handle some of those

growing areas of uncontrolled device interactions, whilst simultaneously opening up more APIs and services?

BYOD

BYOD stands for bring your own device. The acronym really grew into common IAM vernacular, during employee transformation, with staff starting to bring their own mobile phones and tablets into the workplace. The general management of such devices often included the use of endpoint protection systems, certificate infrastructures, access control policies and various different options that allowed organisation controlled data and apps to be sandboxed and separated from personal use.

In a CIAM setting, nearly 100% of all interactions are likely to be with a user who is using their own device—entirely uncontrolled by the service provider. How can the service provider gain some control and why do they want to?

Think of the following scenario: a typical end user with no history of suspicious activity or malicious behaviour logs into an Internet service—perhaps with a username and password and maybe a second factor such as a push notification to a mobile phone. The application on the phone receives the necessary session or access tokens to access downstream systems. However, the end user has also inadvertently downloaded another application from a commercially available application store that happens to contain malware. This secondary application is part of a botnet and is attempting to swamp outbound network connections with ICMP ping packets, or worse.

Device Hygiene

One basic way to overcome similar assurance issues, is to perform some hygiene checks on the end user's device before they interact with the downstream service. This is conceptually similar to workforce network access control, when a device attempted to join the controlled network, they were checked for health, suitability and screening before being allowed to join the local area network. The hygiene check could be accomplished if the end user is accessing the service via a native application and not directly via a web browser. A mobile application can access underlying mobile operating system APIs in order to ascertain certain levels of device assurance. These could include things like hardware characteristics, location data, operating system versions and jailbroken status.

Device Printing

A similar theme to hygiene is device printing. The concept here is to tie a particular user to a device they used during login. A change of device is often seen as a risky event and can trigger counter measures by the service provider–perhaps asking for further information, the sending of a notification email or increased monitoring. The device being bound to the user profile would have gone through the basic hygiene checks to make sure it passes certain criteria regarding assurance, before a fingerprint being taken and saved against the user's profile. Every time the user logs in, a device check is made and compared to previously used devices. On successful validation, a persistent cookie or even certificate could be installed into the device to save further processing in the future.

Devices used for login are not the only kit that an end user may want to interact with in their relations with an online service. The Internet of Things (IoT) has created an entirely new industry of network connected gadgets–ranging from advanced production line monitors and sensors, through to smart televisions and door bells. What impact do they play on a CIAM ecosystem?

★ Device binding is a relatively cheap approach to personalisation and basic security vetting
★ Provide strong notification and consent option with regards to device hygiene checks and data capture
★ Use device printing as a tool to avoid continuous interruption and MFA as necessary

IoT

Constrained

Firstly let us start with some basic definitions of what an IoT device actually is. It is quite common to split devices into two categories: *smart* devices and *constrained* devices.

RFC 7228[118] describes a constrained network node as being "A node where some of the characteristics that are otherwise pretty much taken for granted for Internet nodes at the   time of writing are not attainable, often due to cost   constraints   and/or   physical   constraints   on characteristics such as size, weight, and available power and energy". A basic example could be an automated timetabling system at a bus stop or a sensor on a conveyor belt.

Smart

Conversely a "smart" device could be seen to have a more rounded and less restrictive set of processing and interface capabilities and is more likely to be able to adapt to its network surroundings and context. As we're operating with a CIAM lens, we can focus on examples such as a setup TV box or connected sports goods such as basketballs[119]. The main use case with a smart device is to not only connect the gadget to a network, but also allow that device to take on ownership of an identity, typically with a limited set of capabilities in order to capture data, send data or receive preferences and personalisation details.

In the case of the setup TV box, this could entail the box initialising, being paired to specific user via an out of band process, in order to personalise the TV experience—simple concepts we today expect—such as the storage of viewing history, preferred genres and details on the last paused

118https://tools.ietf.org/html/rfc7228
119https://www.wilson.com/en-gb/explore/labs/basketball/wilson-x

times on particular shows.

Device Pairing

This pairing process brings together some new challenges–even if the devices in question have strong network capabilities, there are still likely to be missing keyboards and screens. IETF standard RFC 8628[120] provides an example of how to use a popular authorization protocol such as OAuth2 in this relatively new device landscape. The main premise is to "pair" the device to a user, via an out of band process. The device communicates to a typically cloud located authorization service asking to be paired. The device receives a short unique code–typically 6 digits in length–and presents the code on a screen, if it has one. The pairing user takes the code and on a separate device such as a mobile or laptop, logs into the cloud based authorization service and enters the code. In the background the device has been polling the cloud service to see if it has been "claimed". Once complete, the device can receive the necessary access tokens, scoped and limited in use, that allows it to pull down user specific information and preferences, essentially acting on the user's behalf. In scenarios where no screen is present, other technologies such as NFC (near field communication) or Bluetooth could be used to pair to a smartphone, or leverage the same local Wifi

120https://tools.ietf.org/html/rfc8628

network to pass pairing information via a mobile app.

- ★ Consider scenarios where a user will need to pair non mobile phone devices to their profile
- ★ Look for standards based ways of providing extended integration
- ★ Consider ways for the end user to revoke access at a time of their choosing

Contextual & Adaptive Access

So far we have only touched on some basic security related use cases, mainly associated with account login. But security really only starts post authentication—when the decisions surrounding what the user can actually do within a system are decided—namely a term known as *authorization*. Again, let us start with some basic definitions, before exploring some industry concepts that are popular in the user access space.

Contextual

The term context, is usually referring to any non-identity data that is used during the authentication and authorization events. Non-identity data can refer to information such as location, IP address, device characteristics such as operating system or browser version, hardware models and so on. Other contextual pointers could include information pertaining to previous behaviour and access—has the user recently changed their password, moved house, transferred vast sums of money? Contextual analysis could also extend to including comparison to other users seen to be similar in terms of expected usage patterns or characteristics–is the event currently undertaken deemed to be unusual as compared to peers? When access control systems encounter ambiguous situations, they typically revert to the "default false" position, restricting access. In workforce scenarios, this may well be acceptable–in a CIAM environment, where a poor user experience is based on access control that is too restrictive, a transaction or even the customer may well be permanently lost. But security is vitable, so is there a better way of handling "no"?

Adaptive

Adaptive access lends itself well to the response that is generated on the back of the contextual analysis. Traditional methods of access control often revolved around a strict adherence to allowing or denying access on the back of subject to object rules analysis. With the advent of more contextually aware systems, the end user is often allowed continual access–but that access can often be restricted to a certain degree based on the results of contextual testing. For example, think of a scenario where a user usually logs on to their online banking account via a previously registered and trusted laptop device. However, they are currently away with work and need to log in via a new device. As the credentials they entered are validated, an MFA may also be triggered. As the device is unknown, perhaps they are only allowed to view their account details and not change anything, or perhaps the session results in increased audit checking or has a lower lifespan. The end user receives a level of service, but not necessarily full access. This starts to follow the paradigm of trust, but verify, whilst simultaneously allowing the end user some freedom to perform limited actions, until assurance can be restored to a higher level. The level of adaptability will vary based on the actions within a particular system, but often follow the *disrupt, degrade, destroy* paradigm.

Contextual and adaptive are fairly generic terms that can be implemented in multiple different ways, depending on the available data streams and design of the underlying systems being protected.

Two concepts that have gained popularity in the last 5 years that use context and adaptivity, are Zero Trust and CARTA . Let us expand on those terms a little, taking into account our new found knowledge surrounding contextual and adaptive access.

Zero Trust

The term Zero Trust–often referred to as Zero Trust Network Architecture (ZTNA)–was seen to originate from the Jericho Forum back in 2007[121], on the publication of a paper focused on deperimeterization of the enterprise. The basic premise was that an organization's network, instead of being built on public untrusted zones and relatively trusted private zones, was becoming more porous. This concept has grown in maturity since then, with Google publishing documentation describing their own internal employee management systems focused on the ZTNA concept, called BeyondCorp[122].

Trust, instead of being solely focused on network location, becomes more implicit, split between the trust of the identity and the trust associated with the device being used. The concept of firewalls still exists, but they are only part of a bigger more layered security approach, with gateways or reference monitors protecting the downstream resources and APIs. Access is assumed to legitimately originate in networks disparate to the resources being accessed, so access control decisions need to leverage the identity, device and associated contextual metadata before coming to an adaptive access decision.

121https://publications.opengroup.org/white-papers/security/jericho-forum/w127
122https://cloud.google.com/beyondcorp

CARTA

A cousin of ZTNA, is a concept known as CARTA[123]–or continuous adaptive risk and trust assessment. CARTA is the brainchild of the analyst firm Gartner. CARTA focuses on the continuous assessment of user activity throughout the entire lifecycle of the user session–by analysing a range of contextual signals to help inform access and authentication decision making. Gartner promotes the focus on "identity corroboration" where signals from internal, external, third and first party sources help to develop trust levels for a user and the associated transactions they wish to perform. These signals could be of a positive or negative contribution, but ideally validated at multiple stages of the user activity–not just at login time for example.

Where a signal reduces assurance in a negative way, the necessary adaptive controls and appropriate levels of friction should be applied, until the risk level can be reduced to a more acceptable level. Gartner also focuses on the continual nature of the validations, the interruptions to the user journey and a movement away from vanilla allow or deny responses.

★ Authentication and authorization decisions should rely on non-identity data signals or sources, from internal, external, commercial and open source feeds

★ Validation should occur at multiple stages of the user session–not just at login time

123https://www.gartner.com/webinar/3891406

★ Access response should be flexible–leveraging concepts such as degradation, disruption, data redaction, rate limiting or alleviated audit and monitoring

Fraud Detection & Management

The use of ZTNA or CARTA style security designs is often a result of a broader security outcome. The most obvious is for organisations to tackle the fraud question–either in the form of better detection or improvement management. Detection rightly or wrongly, is often seen as a point in time event–fraud detection during account creation or during the processing of a high risk event. The management aspect is often focused upon reducing the TCOF–the total cost of fraud. It could be unlikely that an organisation is able to rid themselves entirely of fraudulent activity, so must work towards a situation where fraud detection is balanced by the cost of operational management, investigation and recovery.

Detection techniques ideally should be layered–like most security concepts–and be easily integrated (and replaced) throughout all aspects of the CIAM lifecycle. It is likely that many different point products will require integration, to create a fully orchestrated fraud pipeline.

The fraud analysis pipeline is also likely to leverage parallel processing of different signals or decision points. Some may well be internal using the service providers own historical events tracking systems, whilst other signals could well be commercial and external.

★ Integrate fraud detection at all parts of the user journey
★ Leverage internal and external sources of fraud detection machinery
★ Analyse fraud in the context of overall cost reduction and consider both parallel and sequential processing of fraud signals for efficient coverage

Transactional Authorization

One last topic within this access section, and that is to briefly discuss transactional authorization—or txauth. Txauth is focused upon the additional controls often put in place during high risk events. A high risk event is something that either happens infrequently, or has a material impact if performed by the wrong people or at the wrong time. A simple example could be the adding of a new payee on a current bank account. It is typically not something that happens often, and might incur additional checks and validations if the event originates from an unknown device or perhaps in unusual circumstances.

In such a circumstance, additional friction may be introduced into the user journey—such as the completion of an MFA event. The concept behind txauth, is that the additional friction is event driven, not time driven. After the additional MFA has completed, the user's risk level is unaltered—it has neither increased or decreased—and if they performed the same transaction again, they would need to go through the same barrier again. This is subtly different to "step up" authentication where the session and assurance of the user is often elevated for a period of time. In the case of txauth, the risk "elevation" is limited to a particular event.

- ★ Txauth is useful for introducing mandatory friction on a per event basis
- ★ Txauth is typically not circumvented and limited options are available
- ★ Make the extra validation process modular enough to accommodate roadmap changes that follow technology and user trends

This section was focused upon introducing some concepts associated with post login security–namely authorization leveraging both context and adaptive responses. We will now switch gears and turn our attention to what the user can expect to achieve as a consumer of an online system. First step–profile management.

Profile Management

The creation of an initial user profile as part of the onboarding stage, is often only the foundation of the users data management process. The initial user profile needs to contain at least enough information to make a return journey and re-authenticate–as a bare minimum a username (or email address) and password.

Once information has been used to create a profile, the service needs to provide a way for the end user to view, change and ultimately remove that information.

However, the service provider is likely to need more information over time, as the user and service relationship matures and further exchanges of goods, services and personalised experiences takes place.

Progressive Profiling

Let us start with a basic example to describe the concept of progressive profiling and the role it can take in advanced user onboarding. Let us think of an insurance market aggregation and quotation site. There are multiple layers of functionality the site can perform:

1. Aggregate the most popular car insurance providers in to ranked lists
2. Provide a top 5 list of detailed quotations for a specific user and car combination
3. Allow the submission of a car insurance application
4. Complete renewal reminder and referral discounting

For step 1, this information may well be "publicly" available, in the sense the service provider does not require any registration or authentication to take place, before releasing the information. If we think back to the Onboarding section, they may leverage a transparent or "anonymous" registration process for tracking.

Step 2 is slightly more involved–the relationship develops a little. The end user has indicated they are interested in car insurance (as opposed to pet, home or medical for example) and are interested in a rank. Regardless of how the rank was generated, that could indicate to the service provider a buying signal for insurance by the end user–they want to understand who the market is favouring. At this stage it is likely at least an email address may be needed to get this information, along with a date of birth and car registration number. It is likely the service provider would want the user to return, so may either ask for a password or leverage signup (and future login) from a BYOI provider. This "onboarding" needs to be very simple and fast–the exchange of benefit to the end user is still very small and any unnecessary barrier may result in the user abandoning the query.

By step 3, the end user is signalling to the service provider they are ready to buy and want to receive a personalised quotation via an application process. This process requires substantially more information from the end user–in return for a personalised experience. Here a returning user, via a one click sign in, can provide information at the necessary stages of the application process. It is likely they may want to complete the process over a number of visits, so progress bars, time notifications for each stage and the ability to save and return are essential.

Step 4 is more focused on providing future touch points with the end user in order to look for cross sell opportunities for other products. By offering discounts for referrals, the provider could potentially capture expiry dates for other insurance products if enough trust has been generated and the transaction deemed pleasant enough for the end user.

In the above somewhat simplified example, the progressive profiling aspect can be applied in several ways. Firstly, based on the level of functionality the end user is asking from the service provider. Instead of asking for all the personal and car details required to fulfil step 3 in step 1, they are staged and triggered based on the event progress the end user is up to. This allows for incremental information capture in return for increased benefit to the end user. If they had to provide all the information up front, it's likely they would abandon the journey as the perceived benefit was very low at step 1.

A second way is based on task completion. Step 3 requires multiple blocks of information–perhaps personal (address, date of birth, years of driving experience), vehicle related (registration details, length of car ownership, previous crash history) and circumstantial (number of additional drivers and so on). Instead of asking for all information in one form, this could be broken down and asked at different intervals, each revealing different quote responses.

A final way progressive profiling can be triggered is time based. The time window can be inferred from two basic characteristics–the actual duration between events, or the number of times an event has taken place. An example is the freshness of data being provided to the service provider–often focused upon changeable data such as mobile phone number or post code. If the age of said mobile phone number data is older than 6 months, then prompt during the next login event, to ask if the number is still valid. A similar flow may occur during x-number of logins. After 3 logins—re-verify the service terms and conditions or associated marketing terms are acceptable.

- ★ Capture only the information needed to complete the next immediate task
- ★ Deliver micro notifications and clear affirmative consent capture options
- ★ Leverage time or event based information re-verification

Password Management

In the MFA section we described the issues with password use in general and how most CIAM deployments should look to encourage some form of second factor login method. The fact still remains however, that passwords are by far the most popular authentication option and even if MFA was in place, username and password based initial steps are likely. This brings a few issues to consider.

Password Policy

Password policies are required to help maintain password consistency and security. They are likely to contain measures to uphold the password length, complexity requirements—should it contain letter, numbers, special characters and so on—password age, reset options and dictionary comparison checks. With respect to definition requirements, this largely depends on the security threat model being used. NIST 800-63B provides some basic guidelines as to example password complexity, recommending something between 8-64 characters in length, without any repeating characters or dictionary words. They also recommend a comparison against known breached password lists too. Another aspect to consider is password age—requiring users to reset every 28 days for example. A counterpoint to forced regular changes is that end users could potentially indulge in password reuse, so historical reuse checking may also need to be added to the password policy requirements.

Password Storage

NIST 800-63B provides some guidelines on storage too. At a high level passwords should be stored in a cryptographically hashed format. Hashing is preferable to encryption, in order to avoid the potential for the password storage medium to be accessed and the password decrypted, revealing the plaintext value. Hashing of the password should provide a means for the underlying password value to never be returned back to the plain text value. During login a hash comparison takes place, taking the plaintext password entered during login, creating a hash of that which is in turn compared to the one stored on disk. Hashing of passwords is essential to stop "offline" attacks—where an attacker can perform long time operations on a list of stored passwords in order to crack or reverse engineer them.

NIST 800-63B recommends the use of some hashing and derivation functions such as PBKDF2 (password based key derivation function 2), with specific configuration options such as 32bit salt and iteration count of 10,000.

Reset

At some stage, an end user is going to forget their password and require access to a reset flow. This should ideally be self service driven, to not only reduce operational costs of hosting a call centre infrastructure, but to improve usability too. Clearly a reset flow is essentially an authentication event–and if poorly implemented could result in a malicious attacker locking out a user either literally, or via a malicious user changing their password to an unknown value. If some sort of MFA is in place for standard login events, this should be leveraged for the password change journey, perhaps coupled with a reset link sent via email. This then brings a secondary question, surrounding MFA credential reset or rebind. What happens if a user loses their mobile phone with a OTP generator? These flows whilst not rare, may well be better handled via a physical call centre style interaction to perform real time authentication, to save time developing a complex digital journey. The call centre interaction could leverage voice biometry, account specific knowledge or transaction history checking.

- ★ Password policies are recommend way to create baseline security and consistency checks
- ★ A movement towards increased length and pass phrasing may be preferential to regular changes
- ★ Reset flows are authentication events too and should be protected as such

Delegated Administration

So far within Profile Management, we have focused on steps the end user will take to manage some of their own data–either entering more, editing what they have already submitted, or resetting credentials. In the CIAM landscape, there is also another pattern to consider–that of delegated administration. This can come in many flavours. A simple example is that of family account management–typical in the media or leisure sector–where a single user (perhaps the media account bill payer, or lead name on a holiday) is given responsibility for performing some account management actions for other users.

A couple of simple examples may illustrate the point and we can explain the capabilities that may well need to be developed to accommodate them.

Example 1: Media Service Profiling

> In a media service example, an adult may register for a monthly subscription to a movie channel. Once they register they have the capability to create up to

3 more profiles—including children. Each profile can have their own preferences, history and so on. For a child, the main account holder can create an account, and in turn choose the username the child will log in with. It is likely a child (say under the age of 12) will not have an email address, so all notifications will be sent to the main account holder. The username is likely to be anonymous in nature (for example silverbear10) and easy to remember. The assigned "password" may well be a simple PIN—if the main authentication event takes place using the account holders credentials. The account holder will require delegated administration capabilities to create the profiles, reset PINs and remove profiles once no longer needed.

Figure 4.6 Delegated profile management

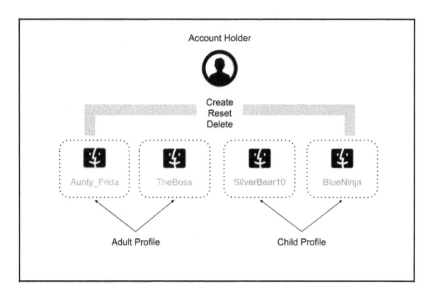

Example 2: Leisure Group Booking

In the leisure industry it is increasingly common to book villa's or even entire package holidays with a group in mind–either for friends or family. A classic process involves a lead passenger name, who would be tagged on all tickets and be the central point of contact for billing and contact via mail. In a digital world, they are more likely to invite other members of the holiday group to participate in the holiday decision process. The lead contact once registered, is likely to have some ability to add multiple other email addresses of their group, to the booking, with each of them receiving a mail inviting them to create a profile and join the booking. Once created they will be able to make micro-decisions for their holiday such as flight seat preferences, holiday activity purchases, day trips and so on. They will likely manage their own password reset process and any payments, without involvement of the booking lead. The entire group access is likely to be time limited–for example 24 hours of the holiday end, all accounts would be automatically disabled or archived.

Figure 4.7 Group invitation management

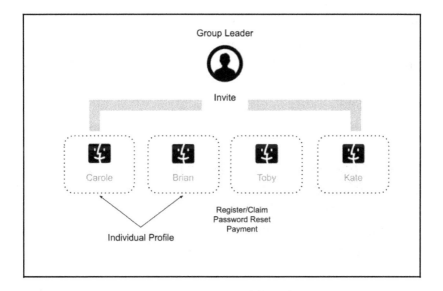

- ★ Identify flows where small self service focused capabilities can be delegated to specific groups
- ★ Family groups are likely to allow for capabilities such as password reset, unlock, or delete
- ★ Invitation and claiming mechanisms are more likely in more formal groupings

So far we have focused the discussion on quite linear user journeys—a task, flow or capability exists and is executed. In reality and especially with regards to more recent compliance initiatives, user consent plays a big part in how those user journeys are constructed.

Consent Management

So where does consent management sit in the CIAM

lifecycle? In the previous chapter we covered a brief look at some of the main external compliance drivers that focus upon end user empowerment–namely the GDPR and CCPA. A key part of consent, is being able to capture user preference, in a way that is transparent and revocable.

Preference Capture

To be able to manage the consent lifecycle, the ability to capture a user's preferences would seem a logical first step. It is important to note what preferences are being asked for and when best to insert the question into the user journey. A modern way to achieve this is via micro-dialogues or interruptions. Preference management should align with the current operation, event or piece of data.

For example, if an email is required for login and the service provider wishes to use that email for secondary purposes such as marketing notifications, at a distinct point in the user journey, a preference interruption should be injected to specifically notify of the intent and provide a clear and modular way for the end user to provide their response. That response should be independent of other uses of the email address. If they decide not to receive marketing notifications via email, that should have no impact on other uses of that value.

The above is a pretty terse and straightforward example of data compliance preferences. What about other preferences–our behaviours are incredibly nuanced and we all have our favourite times of the day, routines, device usage patterns and other concerns which make us all individual. An end user does not necessarily have time to explain those all to a digital and pretty inhumane service that has to cater to millions of requests a day.

Behaviour and Usage

When it comes to data points not necessarily covered by compliance initiatives, end users expect to be informed and involved. They will have preferences when it comes to device, location, presentation and service usage. Let's add some context to this process. For example, say a user is accessing a service via mobile, at 710am in the morning and their geo-location indicates they are likely commuting on a packed train. They would expect the service to "know" they are unlikely to want to read an update to the terms and conditions, see a marketing offer or be bombarded with new and unfamiliar notifications. They are likely to want to login using the same MFA for that time of day and context, receive personalised notifications and have data find them–not the other way around.

The service needs to provide transparent opportunities to model and understand the current context and interrupt only when necessary–and more importantly remember previously provided preferences.

Basic preference interruptions could include the obvious

"remember this device" or "remember this MFA", through to more subtle questions around when future revalidations should occur.

Data Access

A big part of compliance is providing a foundation to capture explicit responses for access to personal data. As we discussed in *chapter 3*, this should occur on a per value basis, as the data is asked for, or when a usage or access request change is being made. There should be an ability to explicitly capture the response (even if negative) in a simple and secure way.

Dashboarding

Any explicitly defined preferences need presenting to the end user in a way that they can easily understand, change and revoke. A centralised dashboard should show all existing preferences that have been explicitly or implicitly made. When it comes to explicit decisions regarding data, the dashboard should contain reference to all previously shared data points, along with basic explanations as to why that data is being held. An explicit revocation action should also be available to remove access to individual data points. The revocation action should also be retrospective–so not just removing future access, but also potentially altering the status of previously shared data.

Implicit behavioural assumptions–most logged in IP

address, most active device, application usage history and so on, should also be available, allowing the end user to delete, edit or download in a manner that is compliant to local data privacy laws.

- ★ Dashboards should be simple to understand and not over power the end user with unnecessary jargon or options
- ★ User interfaces should be blocked to represent different preference and data options, with simple revocation, delete and download capabilities
- ★ The full impact of revocation actions should be made clear

Data Management

So far we have focused our attention on data supplied by the end user in one form or another—essentially information required to authenticate and associated metadata covering their user profile and device usage.

However, there are likely other integration points tied to the user's profile—or an opaque reference belonging to the profile. Those integration points are likely to cover both analytics and usage, through to general marketing and relationship management. Why are they needed?

Before CIAM, the customer was often at the *end* of a marketing and sales funnel. Today, many organisations in pursuit of increased sales or user engagement, leverage concepts such as joint execution plans, where mutually agreed upon targets are set, that both the end user and supplier work towards–the sale, if one exists, is merely part of a longer journey, where the end user is empowered to reach their own goals.

For example–Amazon's immediate use, may well be to allow an end user to purchase a particular item, at the best price, in the simplest and most time effective way possible. But the subtle joint plan is to make the consumer become reliant on them as a platform for ecommerce, groceries entertainment, films, reading and more. So how can they achieve that? By empowering the end user to feel they are partnering with a trusted supplier–"they do what they say, they know me, understand me and are proactive". One sale isn't the goal. Long term stickiness is the goal.

To achieve that level of joint relationship multiple systems are needed, with CIAM the glue that can often link them together.

Integration

Marketing

> Marketing automation systems helps marketers and sales teams to better engage and analyse their user community. It can help marketers drive and manage campaigns, especially with regards to enterprise sales and account based marketing strategies. Marketing automation helps sales by analysing prospect and user behaviour in order to be more

targeted and prepared for joint success planning. Typical marketing activities may include tracking particular web page hits, downloads of particular content and documentation, form filling activity and whether an email was opened and when. So how can CIAM help here? User behaviour plays a big role in marketing automation and as CIAM is the foundation for allowing digital interactions to take place, many organisations devise simple integration processes. These data flows can often be bi-directional. For example tying activity data from an email campaign with CIAM profile data, in order to identify if a previously registered email address is up to date. If multiple mail campaigns were never opened by a particular user, perhaps the next time they log in, leverage progressive profiling to verify their email address is correct. Conversely, data from the CIAM login and transaction process could be sent into the marketing automation system to help understand which services are being used at what time, location and device in order to improve customer support.

Analytics

A close cousin to the marketing automation system, is that of user analytics. There are a few threads to user analytics. The first are the analytics embedded within the CIAM tasks themselves—login journeys, access request processes and reset flows. The second more tangential focusing on web page or application usage. Within the CIAM journey compendium, analytics really add value to understanding the most optimal user, reset and registration flows. Analytics is focused typically on metrics and timers, helping to answer questions such as:

- How long does the new fingerprint biometric login take versus OTP?
- Does a password reset journey of more than 5 steps result in a help desk call?
- If a login journey takes over 10 seconds, does that result in increased abandoned shopping cart instances?
- How many users in North America are using iPhone 5's or newer?
- Is Android more popular in APAC than in Europe?

That level of detail can help improve MFA rollout choices, reduce friction during key authentication and authorization journeys and help to increase security, by identifying weak device assurance cases. Integration to journey based analytics may simply come from server side analysis—perhaps via logging systems. Other approaches could leverage the hashing of user identifiers and embedding client side libraries within browsers that associate application specific behaviour with pseudo anonymous analysis.

Customer Data Platform

A third area of popular integration, that often brings together both marketing automation and user analysis, is that of the customer data platform (CDP) or customer relationship management (CRM) suite. Whilst they could be distinguished separately, many argue they are the same thing. The main concept behind them being different systems, is often the distinction of anonymous and known users and automated and manual data capture—with a CDP being able to focus on anonymous and automated too. For the sake of discussion, we will assume a central tool that focuses on the sales operation pipeline, and developing a single view of customer interactions.

A typical mantra of CDP deployment is that the customer becomes more central to all marketing, sales and post sales activities—essentially a customer centric flywheel. This helps to support the joint execution plan approach. A CDP's main goal is often to reduce silo's—so the linkage of data from the user authentication profile, analytics and marketing behaviour becomes critical—often keyed off pseudo anonymous identifiers linked back to the CIAM identity.

The CDP is the main entry point into customer data management and analytics, with static and real time data updates from multiple systems including campaign response data from marketing and any analytics and tracking data captured at run time.

Figure 4.8 Sample data integration scenario

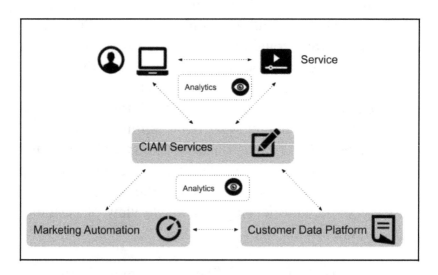

The CIAM service integration is likely to be bi-directional, leveraging connectors and standards based APIs based on REST and JSON. We will cover integration protocols in more detail in *chapter 7.*

- ★ Consider bi-directional data sharing across a multitude of different business focused systems
- ★ Keep the CIAM services repository light and containing only "just enough information to authenticate"
- ★ Leverage standards based connectors and integration points such as APIs for easy implementation and future proofing

User Data Sharing

Generated data also needs sharing. Depending on what that data is and where it originated, it may well need sharing too. In an employee focused IAM landscape data access control policy would be managed by IT administrators. They would define a policy that governs which users (subjects) can access which systems (objects), sometimes along with the entitlements or actions too. In a CIAM landscape, the consumer is the centre of the flywheel, so all surrounding systems must put them central too. In the case of data sharing, the end user should be the one who controls access to their data.

This user centric access control process is slightly different to just capturing for user preferences. We now need to concentrate on run time data too. For example, how can we start to answer questions like the following:

- How can a patient actively share health care records, scans and x-rays to trusted physicians or insurance providers?
- How can the owner of a fitness tracking wearable, share their hiking data with a third party cloud service to monitor weight loss?
- How can the driver of a smart car share maintenance details with an insurer?

These sorts of interactions are above and beyond the concepts fixated with IT centric policy control. The data is dynamic, the access could be just-in-time and the data owners could scale into their thousands if not millions in a single deployment.

User Managed Access

A protocol to tackle these sorts of problems is called UMA[124]–or user managed access. As the name implies, the *user* is the entity managing the access control process not the system administrator. Based upon OAuth2–another standard we will cover in more detail in *chapter 7*–UMA aims to provide a generic set of principles that allows for the sharing of virtually anything to trusted third parties–either in advance (Alice wants to share a photo with Bob) and in retrospective too (Bob requests access to Alice's photo, and then Alice has a decision to make in response).

A key part of data sharing is revocation. This can generate lots of nuanced workflows. How can a CIAM system answer questions like the following:

- What would trigger a data revocation flow? Is the revocation manual or automatic?
- What happens to previously shared data once access has been removed? Is the data also removed?
- Does the central sharing authority require notification that previously accessed data has been removed?

In the case of run time or streaming data, this may be less

124https://kantarainitiative.org/confluence/display/uma/Home

of an issue–but relatively static data such as health care records, may require more prudent revocation workflows.

Another user sharing aspect to consider, is that of temporal access. This could be literal in the case of a user assigning time limits to the receiver or more logic based. For example, Dr Smith can only access x-rays whilst the patient is under care, or perhaps access to fitness wearable GPS data is only available in certain geolocations during a competitive event.

★ Considers data points which are likely to incur using sharing requests
★ Leverage standards based approaches for developing user centric sharing protocols
★ Analyse data revocation workflows and remediation

Privacy Preservation

Not only does the CIAM lifecycle require a user centric sharing (and revocation) framework to be in place, it is quite likely that the lower level operations of getting data from place to another, will require additional privacy preservation steps.

Privacy and security often get intermingled. Privacy is typically associated with the confidential protection of personal identifiable information or PII. Secrecy is associated with system level protection mechanisms upholding confidentiality. So whilst privacy may focus upon masking data fields and creating per transaction sharing agreements, the secrecy aspect may fulfil those requests over confidential channels.

Let us take a brief look at some data privacy mechanisms that are likely candidates for inclusion in the broader CIAM data ecosystem.

Masking

> The basic premise of masking, is to essentially hide specific fields (or parts of fields) within a data object, whilst not restricting too much the usefulness of the underlying data to the consuming system. An example could include removing parts of a person's date of birth, leaving only the year or perhaps blanking out 12 of 16 digits in a credit card number. The process for the masking could include functions such as hashing (a non-reversible cryptographic process), nullification (replacement with empty characters), obfuscation (character replacement with symbols such as–or #) or basic shuffling and substitution. How and when the masking takes place could vary–it could occur for all data, dynamically at run time, or perhaps based on the context of the queries being made against the original data set.

Tokenization

> Tokenization is another form of data hiding, but this time it is more reversible and deterministic. The

concept behind tokenization, is that sensitive fields (or parts of) are replaced with a non-sensitive reference. The new non-sensitive representation can be stored or transferred to systems that have less assurance associated with them. Upon use of the non-sensitive value, an application could call a tokenization service that would essentially swap the substituted value for the original for processing. Some nuances with tokenization exist—namely format preservation. Again if we take credit card numbers as an example, they exist in a 16 digit form. So the tokenized version must also exist in a 16 digit format. Whilst encryption or hashing methods could be used, it is important to note the output length and format of those processes may need altering or restricting in order to resemble the original form. This allows downstream systems to store and process the tokenization format as they would with the original value.

Homomorphic Encryption

One final area to touch upon when it comes to privacy preservation, is a relatively more recent area called homomorphic encryption. The concept is to allow untrusted third parties to process and analyze sensitive data—without having access to the original values. The data is encrypted in a way that allows queries, analysis and other processing to occur, with the results being the same as if the processing occurred on the original unencrypted values. This is a valuable concept, especially in areas such as healthcare research. There are different levels of homomorphic encryption, depending on the types of calculations that are to be performed on the encrypted data–commonly known as being *somewhat* homomorphic, *partially* homomorphic and *fully* homomorphic encrypted (FHE). As this area is relatively new, the https://homomorphicencryption.org/ body aims to promote standardization, with participants from the likes of Microsoft, Google and Intel amongst others.

★ Focus beyond just security of data at rest and consider how data in *use* could impact decisions regarding privacy management
★ Isolate data consumers and how they interact with original sources of sensitive data
★ Analyse data format and the limitations many applications may have with respect to how they process data

Account Removal

The last focus area within the CIAM lifecycle, is that of account removal. An often forgotten about topic, but one which can generate numerous functional requirements.

At some point, an end user will no longer require access to a service they have registered for. The origins for that could either be service side or end user related. For example, the end user could simply register for a competitive service. The service provider on the other hand, many terminate access to a service if payment has been missed or a breach in usage terms has occurred.

Not all routes to termination are the same and not all termination outcomes will be equal either. Depending on the level of downstream integration, there will be considerable clean up operations that will need to take place. Let us take a look at some core CIAM service related functionality that should exist, followed by a couple of simple example termination flows.

Disabling

An obvious immediate step in a removal process is account disabling. This is useful for several reasons. It immediately prevents use of the account–both from the actual and malicious user perspective. Malicious user activity on dormant accounts may well be more difficult to identify, mainly as the actual user may no longer receive notifications or observe unusual behaviour. Disabling the account, typically by a flag on the user profile, can simply prevent login for everyone. Disabling is also temporary and can be easily reversed and subsequently allow secondary processing of integrated systems.

Account Reuse Prevention

When a user no longer has access to a system, it

could seem obvious to simply remove their account from the system. This has several implications. Firstly, for some compliance and reporting reasons, having the necessary audit reports showing the account existed is essential. Removal of the physical account and underlying identifier may subvert that process. A secondary aspect is account reuse prevention. For example, say a user created an account with username "Bob2020", subsequently requested account termination and the username was removed. Could that allow an entirely different user the ability to re-create a user with the username "Bob2020"? If so, could they then start to represent that user within any associated communities? Yahoo email had a similar situation occur in 2013[125], when the recycling of old email addresses was introduced. Even if an account is disabled and subsequently removed at some point, the re-use of the same usernames and identifiers should be restricted.

Account Data Download

Account data download is not just associated with the account removal process, but the ability for the end user to download their profile and associated data often occurs during this time. As a key part of initiatives such as the GDPR, the end user should always have the right to download any data the service provider holds about them. This data should

125https://www.theverge.com/2013/9/24/4765988/yahoo-users-report-security-problems-with-recycled-email-addresses

be formatted in an industry standard way, such as CSV or JSON and not require any proprietary tools to view or manage. The time to process such as a data download request should be reasonable too, and easy to trigger from an end user perspective.

Archiving

Archiving is often a process that occurs a set period of time period after account disabling. The archive process typically sees the movement to secondary storage systems of user login profiles and any associated data. This reduces load and storage costs on run time systems and allows for cleaner demarcation for long term processing.

Data Tokenization

During archiving, data may well be tokenized, or entirely shredded using cryptographic processes. Personally identified fields should be masked or nullified, whilst log data may undergo a process of tokenization. Log entries may still exist pertaining to login, logout and activity events, but the data tying the activity back to a physical entity may need to be removed. If data is encrypted using keys attributed to a specific identity, those keys may well need deleting, in order to essentially remove any access to data, whilst leaving the data in place for auditing or reporting processes.

Data Removal

Finally a data removal process will exist–but essentially only at the end of a chain of correctly executed, disabling, archiving and shredding processes.

Figure 4.9 Example user initiated removal process

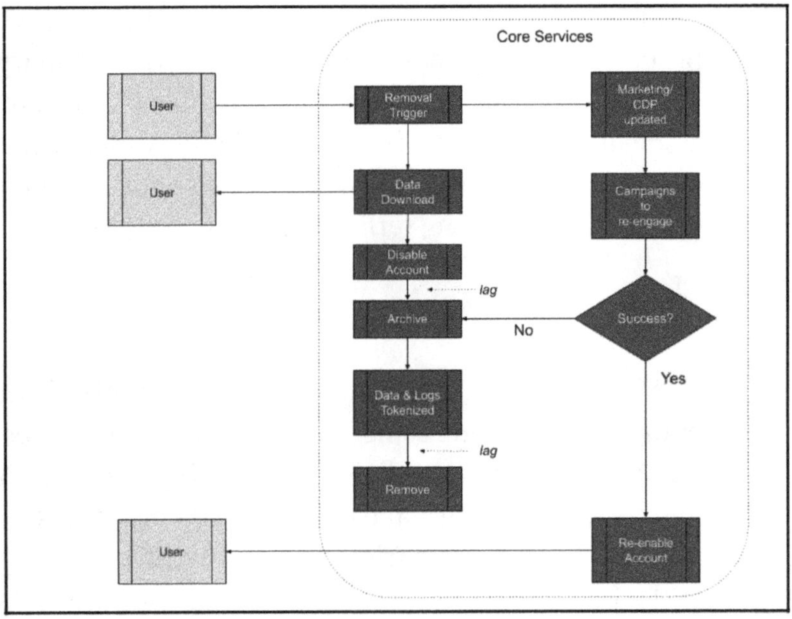

* ★ Provide a simple means for end user to start the removal process via self service
* ★ Be cognizant of compliance processes for data download, tokenization and removal processes
* ★ Prevent reuse of identifiers or other persona based capabilities

Summary

This chapter introduced the concept of the CIAM lifecycle–a set of example steps and associated functional components, that a user will likely go through when it comes to interacting with an online service.

The key takeaway is that the CIAM service layer will contain multiple different functions that interact with multiple downstream systems–either to protect and interact with, or to act as a bi-directional data vehicle.

In the next chapter, we will focus upon design planning–how to analyse requirements and ask the right questions to help build a set of CIAM focused services.

CHAPTER 5

Design Planning

This chapter will focus upon providing guidance during the CIAM design planning phase. Like any project, it is important to identify the key requirements before embarking on the build and delivery phases. Think of the Design Planning stage as "problem setting"–working out what needs building–whereas later stages, such as Solution Planning are more focused upon *how* to build.

There are numerous great resources focused on project management and planning and I don't want to delve too deep into concepts such as Waterfall or Agile project management. The Association of Project Management[126] amongst others, can provide a great overview of the differing project management options that are available. Many CIAM projects are likely to fall under an Agile approach for implementation–typically due to the transformative nature of the resulting project. Agile is also quite likely in CIAM projects where the future outcomes or success criteria might not always be clear.

Business Objectives Mapping

As we discussed in *chapter 1*, CIAM is typically an outside-in set of flows–attracting and managing entities that

---

126https://www.apm.org.uk/resources/what-is-project-management/what-is-a-life-cycle/

typically reside *outside* of the organisation, in order to deliver goods, services and applications that reside *inside*. To allow for such cross-functional operations to take place, a business focused set of objectives need to be created and disseminated.

But what does that mean? CIAM is not a technology lead component. It relies on objectives that are centered around how the entire business (or product) is to focus, how the success metrics are defined and what any associated mission and vision statements define.

A CIAM project designer needs to understand the direction of the travel for the business area they are working in. This will entail working with key stakeholders inside the business to help understand current short and long term themes, as well as analysing externally, what the market threats, opportunities and trends could be.

Understanding the business direction helps to provide guidance as to what key CIAM related problems need solving—not necessarily when they need solving, but helping to identify that they exist.

For example, if a shoe retailer has analysed its last three years of sales activity and identified that year on year growth is shrinking, a strategic objective could be to increase revenue via an online store front, whilst simultaneously cutting costs by closing physical stores and transitioning staff into a new digitally focused fulfilment unit. How could CIAM help here? Well clearly a digital store would need functionality that allows an individual to purchase items–and an identity based sales portal could help in order to help drive repeat sales via personalised interactions, fashion tips and sales help. But that one sentence is full of nuanced detail.

- Should the digital storefront focus on new customers or existing customers from the old physical store front?
- If existing–what demographic, purchase trends and other metadata is available?
- If new–will they replace or augment existing customers? What target market is being aimed at?
- What does success look like? Will the storefront replace all existing physical revenues?
- What timelines are important?
- Are there any existing digital shoe stores in the market?

The key takeaway–is to ask questions. A lot of questions. It is vitally important to unearth the real underlying business goals before attempting to design some of the key CIAM requirements. Unlike technically lead projects, CIAM should be rooted in helping to achieve really high level business objectives. For example, subtle changes in the registration process could dramatically alter the target demographic for net-new shoe consumers, which in turn would have a profound impact on the overall business objective.

Starting with the end in mind, is also a useful and critical tool when helping to understand the business direction. An example of this, could include defining the CIAM product launch email or press release that would be issued once the project goes live. This may seem like an odd exercise, but actually helps to solidify what the solution is aiming to achieve, who is set to benefit and any associated success factors.

The point of a press release document, can help to create a "not todo" list. When developing any new service or solution, larger themes are likely to be identified, which will need breaking down into smaller bite sized stories. It can be very easy to lose sight of the long term objective and prioritise lots of individual tasks against each other. By focusing on a more succinct end goal—which a press release is a basic aim towards—can help to keep in check changing demands, and incremental requirement changes.

There are numerous templates[127] that exist for a press release product launch, but many will include items such as a snappy headline, a lead (that describes the who, what, why, when and with what effect), a detailed body explaining the lead as well as information surrounding the company or product position. In many respects the CIAM project is no different to any other product launch, except it can have a fundamental bearing on the business success.

★ Analyse and understand the overarching objectives of the business via interviews and documented mission and vision statements

[127]https://prowly.com/magazine/new-product-press-release-examples/
#product-line-example

- ★ Perform a basic "five-whys" questioning of immediate strategic aims
- ★ Identify key stakeholders and what success metrics they are using

Stakeholder Analysis

The business objectives mapping, is likely to help reveal who the main interested parties in the CIAM project are likely to be. In most organisations, depending on structure, is likely to include the CMO (chief marketing officer), the CISO (chief information security officer), CIO (chief information officer) and a representative from the identity community—likely an architect or product services owner.

Under those four pillars, are likely to be sub teams and personnel who will have specific objectives surrounding concepts such as customer or user happiness, retention, call centre contact reduction and so on.

Let us analyse some basic examples of what each of the four pillar leaders will be looking for with regards to their input into the design phase.

CMO

The CMO is going to be focused on the initial user onboarding and acquisition phase of the CIAM lifecycle. Questions they are likely to want answered will be aimed at the registration process—how that can be customized to attract users from particular demographics, age groups, personas and the like. The registration process is a subtle step and requirements for concepts such as theming, branding and multi-device usage will be likely. It is important to dig deep into understanding who the CMO is aiming the registration process at and what usability requirements will be acceptable to particular personas. Security requirements may also be questioned heavily in the CMO discussions, mainly as concepts such as MFA could be seen as being restrictive or complicated and acting as conceptual barriers to service adoption and sign on.

CIO

The CIO is likely focused on the main infrastructure and operational aspects of deployment. Expect to discuss requirements centered around the location of new services and infrastructure—will they be cloud located, data centered located and managed by internal or external teams? The level of customisation versus commercial software will also be a keen topic, as will items focused on future-proofing and road mapping considerations. That in turn will generate demands to understand the existing level of support and engineering capabilities—will new skills, hires or consultants be needed to implement and support any future CIAM components? Understanding what metrics the CIO will be measured against is important of course, and may well touch on areas such as the time to roll out new services, outage and availability statistics and the utilisation of existing specialist personnel and developers.

CISO

The CISO and CIO will be closely related, with the former being more focused on the general security and privacy requirements of the new provisioned service.

An immediate focus for the CISO will be the compliance requirements any CIAM system could generate. We have touched upon the likes of the GDPR and CCPA, but other local requirements may also exist. Will this generate the need for new practices and personnel? The collection of consumer data should clearly be minimised and the CISO will be focused on understanding which pieces of data are required and for what purpose. Detailed data pipelines will need creating, outline the location and service processors that will act upon collected information. Basic service functions such as allowing end user editing and removal of collected data will also need to be designed with input from the CISO lead community.

Identity Architect

The identity team will be focused on automating as many of the identity related data flows as possible, using either commercial of custom solutions. Service descriptions for components such as MFA, authorization, end user profiling and application onboarding will be of interest to the identity team. Identifier discussions—such as whether to use usernames, globally unique identifiers or email addresses—will be paramount and how data from other systems will be linked together. The identity team is also going to be in pole position to own policy and control material centered around password complexity, device hygiene analysis, lock out policies, reset policies and notification and auditing.

In general with respect to stakeholder engagement and analysis:

- ★ Identify the main stakeholders from the key executive team pillars
- ★ Engage via interviews, questionnaires and existing process review
- ★ Correlate and contrast high level component requirements, identifying early areas of conflict and quick wins

What Are You Building? (And For Whom?)

After a period of analysis understanding the main high level business or departmental objectives, the various stakeholders interested in the project should be easily identifiable. Based on those discussions, a high level view of what needs building and for whom. There is a clear distinction between "what" to build, versus "how" to build. Many projects often start too early with the how, and engage engineering and development teams without a fully fledged design that articulates the main problem that needs fixing.

The role of designer (or product manager/owner) is to be able to represent the voice of the end user or consumer –and be their advocate. It is important to be able to describe the problem to be fixed, more than the solution that is being created. The solution is typically a lot easier to articulate (and in turn faster to deploy) if the true underlying problem is well understood.

We started this chapter with a reference to "starting with the end" in mind—and that is a key dogma in helping to articulate what is being built and for whom. By being very clear, in simple terms, what is being built, what problem it will solve and whom it will benefit will make solution design and any associated engineering tasks much easier.

A basic value proposition should start to develop after the initial discussions. This value proposition should aim to cover the following structure:

- The *Who*—who is the solution for?
- The *Need*—describe what they need
- The *What*—high level service description
- The *Difference*—how it is unlike existing / competitive approaches
- The *Impact*—how it helps the consumer

The above can be a little confusing at first. Think of a made up example like the following to put it into context. This is aimed at a new service for our shoe retail company we discussed earlier.

- For the time constrained office professional
- Who need smart, fashionable footwear
- The ACME shoe store portal, is a personalised

digital shoe store that provides tailored shoe recommendations
- Unlike physical shoe fitting services that are limited in choice
- Our product allows a proactive try before you buy subscription that reduces buy time and cost

A very simple template like the above can help to focus attention on the "not todo" versus an ever growing list of todo's, and backlog items. By simply articulating what is being built for whom, allows an initial design–or minimal viable product–to focus attention and develop an immediacy of value driven wins.

If the aim of service adoption is on the "time constrained office professional", focus the registration on being completed during office commutes for example, where mobile devices and limited attention span will be common.

If a tailored experience is important, what information is needed during onboarding? Perhaps not a full user life history, but limit to age, sex and and some examples of their fashion style.

If the end user has avoided physical stores in the past, there is limited need to replicate the physical storefront online–instead focus upon digital experiences they are already familiar with. Leverage "swipe and deploy" tactics from other online store fronts–media, music or film and develop a narrative on their existing experiences.

Personalisation and proactivity seem key, so the ability to collect feedback, offering of choice and allowing for changes to preferences should be embedded in the design concepts from an early stage–allowing for modularity of key components to allow for rapid change and A/B testing.

Where possible, also apply some objective success metrics to each of the persona outcomes. At this early phase, that may seem difficult as the data may not always be available. If the aim in this basic example is to attract the "time constrained professional", are there statistics around how large that user community is? What percentage of that community do you want to attract to the new service? Is that time bound–so 5,000 on week one, ramping to 50,000 by month 3? Metrics are not only good for delivering a message of success (or failure) to senior management, but they can also help with the iterative development process, applying the captured feedback to the next phase of decisions.

★ Focus a value proposition on a particular user persona
★ Identify how a new service would make a difference to the selected user community
★ Help to create "not do" lists as opposed to opening up the opportunity for ever growing backlogs with no priority compass

Design Principles

Before embarking on solution implementation it is important to have a focused list of principles regarding some of the key non-functional aspects of the CIAM project. Many of these core components may be inherited from other parts of the organisation's technology strategy. Some organisations and governments publish their overarching technology design principles. An example from the UK, is their Government Digital Service[128], which outlines how they tackle the delivery of their citizen services transformation programme.

It can be helpful to explicitly state these principles in order to help articulate what should *not* be built.

Security

> From a design planning perspective, will the new CIAM system open new attack vectors? Very likely and may introduce new approaches to work (agile), new personnel (digital designers) and new systems (CIAM platform)–all of which will impact the organization's security posture. It should be critical that any new service should not reduce the security posture of the organisation or existing service.

Privacy

> The compliance demands on a CIAM project are likely to be considerable, with regards to how PII is collected, stored and processed. If the organisation is not within the financial services sector, this may introduce new procedures and concepts. With all

128https://www.gov.uk/guidance/government-design-principles

new pieces of collected data required to fulfil the CIAM service, there needs to be documented justification and a clear end to end lifecycle description of how that data should be handled. If any stakeholder requests new data to be collected, they need to justify it.

Scalability

CIAM services may result in user volumes into the hundreds of thousands or millions. What can be difficult is to predict the actual expected user numbers, making initial capacity planning more complex than employee focused IAM systems. Any changes to functionality and target audience should be analysed to understand usage impacts, with maximum high water marks tested throughout the infrastructure.

Elasticity

A cousin to scalability, is that of elasticity. Any identified changes to functionality, target audience or context, may result in the need to rapidly expand capacity and in turn reduce capacity after a peak capacity has taken place. The underlying service infrastructure should allow for expansion and reduction (ideally automatically) without impact on the end user experience.

Pluggable & Extendable

CIAM aims to solve numerous digital transformation related problems–many related to solving complex and sometimes unknown problems. Digitization is a concept heavily embedded with continual change. A CIAM based system needs to cater for future roadmapping, unknown changes, integrations and technology evolutions. Extension and pluggability can help cater for changes and customization–and these should be handled as business as usual tasks not as re-engineering.

Standards Support

Standards help to drive interoperability, could arguably improve code design and technology (due to the large peer review process standards often go through) and help reduce time to solve complex problems. There are many standards related to CIAM base functionality that can help deliver many functions for "free", as the heavy lifting of innovation and design has already been done. This allows engineers who perhaps are not domain experts, to follow well designed APIs and protocols. Where possible when introducing new capabilities, research the existence of industry standards that may already deliver the necessary functionality.

Resilience & Recovery

One of the key components of delivering an external Internet facing system, is that it will typically be accessible at all times, unlike internal employee systems which would always have quiet or maintenance periods. Whilst availability is not directly the same as resilience and recovery, any developed services need to consider the ability to not only avoid denial of service, capacity or throughput constraints, but also have mechanisms to shed or transfer load, gracefully degrade and recycle their service delivery mechanisms.

Having a basic set of design principles, can help to focus on how to implement certain requirements, but also focus on what not to do. If a requirement is raised that doesn't fulfil the privacy workflow, or perhaps introduces a bespoke piece of data handling that doesn't scale, that should raise alarm bells as falling outside the basic principles of the CIAM design.

Summary

The main takeaway in this chapter is simple: understand the problem before embarking on the solution. It is key to understand how the CIAM based solution or service, will empower the business to fulfil its growth objectives. Work with key stakeholders, understand their individual requirements before working against a set of basic design principles to help create a set of measurable components that can be solutionized.

Chapter 6 will take a slightly more fine grained look at some of the next stage functional requirements.

CHAPTER 6

Solution Planning

This chapter will focus upon providing more lower level guidance on some of the concepts identified in *chapter 5.* Here we move away from high level discovery and take a look at some individual functional requirements and how to ask the right questions to uncover more detailed features.

User Coverage

The CIAM system is unlikely to be seen as successful, if it has no users using it. It is important when designing such systems, to understand who will use it, when they use it, why and how.

For internal IAM focused systems, those requirements are often not too detailed for several reasons. Firstly employee focused identity is largely focused on employees. An obvious statement that delivers some pretty large assumptions. Firstly until quite recently, employees accessed internal systems using company managed desktops, laptops and tablets. The last few years has certainly seen the rise of BYOD to the workplace, but even BYOD support is often managed via agents or applications that can provide management functions and sandboxing within the device. If the employee is to access an organisationally managed system, they will typically do so via a high level of organisational control. Secondly, when they do so it is relatively well controlled and operates within quite a narrow window–namely "office hours" with some exceptions.

The zero trust paradigm, of not trusting request origin location and exposing more services and APIs to users accessing from non-controlled environments, is akin in many respects to a CIAM system. In a CIAM powered service, you are exposing functionality to a relatively uncontrolled set of users. If we continue the shoe shop example from *chapter 5*, any new shoe customer could use the new online service. You may aim for certain target demographics, but consumers will come in all shapes and sizes, with different preferences, devices, levels of experience and levels of service expectation. Somehow the CIAM system has to cater for the vast majority and do so consistently.

With respect to user coverage it is important to try and break down the expected user community. Try and think of being able to answer questions like the following:

- What age and sex of users are being targeted?
- Where will the users be located? What geographies?
- Will they be using laptops, mobiles or tablets?
- What makes and models of mobile devices?
- What information is available regarding operating system coverage for the mobiles in those regions?
- What time of day and what days of the week will be most popular?

Some of this information may well be available from the

high level design. The CMO will clearly have a target market of who they want to attract and register for the new service. Secondary detail may well be a research exercise. For example, different geographies will see more popular mobile operating systems than others, with different versions being run. That information if likely available via vendor and operator reports or paid for market research.

Usage pattern information may well be unknown until the system is launched. If so it is important to be able to capture and analyse such information when the system is live. Being able to see that 55% of users authenticated between 8-10pm on a weekend via Android, can not only help from a security analytics perspective, but also via personalised experience and new feature launch planning too.

User coverage will also have some fundamental impacts on things like service level agreements and help desk support. If the user community has a large age range (say 10-80 years of age for media content viewing), the device supportability matrix will be quite large. Not all 80 year olds will be using the most recent version of an Apple phone and will likely require different support processes for things like MFA enrollment failure or password reset. Indeed would they be comfortable with using an MFA function such as fingerprint?

By broadening the user coverage net, the number of potential users of the service may well increase. However, it is important to consider the marginal cost of each new user community that signs up.

This marginal cost barrier is not just related to age. Think of the following user community characteristics in *figure 6.1* and the associated design or support options that may need to be considered.

Figure 6.1 User community examples with marginal cost challenges

User Community Characteristic	Potential Design Cost
English is not a first language	Language localization of interfaces and apps; ability to store different character sets in the backend databases
EU citizens	Compliance requirement support such as GDPR
Under 16 years of age	Increased privacy regulation
Prevalence of older / second hand mobile devices	Increased security vulnerabilities; support for multiple application versions; increased testing costs
Early technology adopter	Feature delivery infrastructure and process that delivers quick releases

Total control over the user community will be impossible but it is important to know some basic characteristics of the initial targeted user base.

Application Coverage

Another main difference with employee IAM is that the application coverage of a CIAM system is often quite narrow. Employee application integration may well be quite broad and deep, requiring complex permissions management, application onboarding and governance. In the CIAM world, the access and onboarding aspect with regards to application integration is likely to be quite shallow. The number of applications is likely to be smaller and the level of complexity of those applications on the front end at least considerably lower.

The back end support–perhaps in the form of microservices or APIs–may well be more complex, but often that complexity is abstracted away from the end user functions.

Let us split the coverage question then, into two parts: front end user facing and back end fulfilment.

Front-end

> The front-end will essentially be the user interfaces and applications that deliver data and expose functionality directly to the user of the service. To that end user, the front-end *is* the application. This will be the place they register, login and consume services, make purchases or perform transactions. As with any system, usability, simplicity and reduction of complexity, will be vitality important to

ensure a satisfying user experience. However with regards to CIAM, there are some additional subtleties that need to be considered as part of the design. One is regarding single view and signal sign on. As with employee based identity, it is important to reduce the number of times a user has to authenticate to fulfil a particular function. For example, say you are developing a retail banking application. This application could deliver a range of different pieces of functionality from viewing bank balances, cashing in rewards points, adding standing order payees or modifying monthly payments. Under the covers, that may require a myriad of different systems to fulfil those different functions, but from an end user standpoint, they only see a single bank—so in turn they do not expect to login four times to 4 different systems in order to complete a range of tasks they could complete in a single visit to a bank's physical branch.

An extension to that single sign on process, is the legitimate case of a single entity delivering multiple brands with distinct applications and front-end interfaces. This can be quite common during mergers and acquisitions, or for organisations where different brands are created for different regions, products or communities. Whilst branding and logical separation is important, from an end user perspective, if they are consumers of multiple brands, they may expect to perform functions in one application after successfully authenticating into another.

Back-end

The backend APIs, systems and databases required to support functionality in the front-end are likely to be considerable. They are likely to be highly interdependent and reliant on existing data sources and functions. The design of backend systems is likely to be focused on the blast radius of data usage and processing. Even if regulatory compliance is not required, the handling of PII and related sensitive data needs to be done in secure and privacy preserving ways, with well documented data pipelines outlining where data is going and why. Questions will also need answering with regards to how far down the back-end application chain does the end user identity need to go. For example, if John Doe logs into an application and receives the necessary access tokens or cookies, do those tokens need to be presented to layer 2, 3 and 4 APIs that are performing quite low level processing? It is quite likely token exchanges, validation gateways and various different ways of passing the necessary claims would be necessary in order for secondary systems to know the reason and details of the data requests they are presented with. What those systems need to perform their processing would be considerable interest to a back-end designer.

Application integration from a CIAM perspective, is likely

to be considerably smaller, yet at times equally complex in comparison to employee IAM. The number of applications will be lower, but how services are integrated to deliver seamless experiences, single sign on and privacy preserving processing will require a solid end to end understanding of the data lifecycle.

Data Management

One of the big challenges for back-end application processing, will be that of processing CIAM and CIAM related data. What data is being collected, how it will be processed, shared and stored will all require analysing and documenting.

Data is everywhere and CIAM shouldn't generate too many new surprises with respect to data handling. However, CIAM data is often broken down into distinct characteristics which can result in differences in how that data is handled.

JEITA–Just Enough Information To Authenticate

Another acrocryn, this time focused on the user profile. This profile is basically the skeleton of the user using the CIAM service. The profile is likely to contain many pieces of information to make the service operate, but at a minimum, will contain "just enough information to authenticate"–aka a username and password. The username could be an email address, or perhaps for services that want to provide a persona based approach, a user chosen identifier. Other operational attributes may also be needed, such as:

- Attribute to capture active/inactive status
- Last login time
- Last password change time
- Account verification tags–such as emailVerified

It is important to consider how authentication events will govern what basic information is required for registration and future self-service related tasks such as password reset, OTP enrollment and so on. We will touch on authentication in the next section, but it is highly likely that username and password authentication will not be sufficient. If secondary factors are required, it is likely that additional metadata would need to be stored. This could include OTP seeds, device information regarding hardware tokens and public key information if challenge response approaches such as WebAuthn are being used.

It is important to also analyse where this profile information will be stored. It is likely this will need to be stored in a high scale (both capacity of user profiles and access throughput) directory or database.

Further analysis at this stage should focus on questions such as:

- What schema attributes are needed on the basic JEITA profile?

- Where will that information be stored?
- Is there an existing directory or database that can be used?
- What throughput and scale requirements exist?
- How will front-end applications integrate with the back-end repository?
- Does the information need replicating to different geographic regions?
- What aging and archiving strategies are needed?

The JEITA questions of course, only focus on the minimum data specifics regarding how a user logs into the service.

Further integration analysis would need to focus on the storage of preference data, application activity linking, CRM, marketing and other third party system references and pointers.

Some preference data may well sit on the profile store used for authentication. This may include basics around MFA preference and so on. Some profile stores may be extended to include preferences related to terms and conditions and marketing notification, but not all.

Orthogonal systems such as marketing activity tracking, may link via a unique attribute stored on the authentication profile, such as an application specific GUID–or globally unique identifier. This may depend on the privacy requirements regarding interaction analysis. For example downstream marketing systems, may operate against relatively anonymous application specific identifiers and not on items such as names or email addresses.

CRM systems are likely to house more personal contact related information as well as potential linked to payment and invoicing data.

- ★ Identify the basic schema attributes required to login a user
- ★ What replication or geolocation constraints may exist?
- ★ Follow existing password hashing algorithms and identify additional PII that may need encrypting or tokenizing

Authentication

Whilst the user profile is likely to store JEITA, what the authentication process looks like will vary hugely. It is recommended that an MFA of some sort be used, at least for high risk events, but ideally for all interactions. While at first, this may seem to introduce a barrier to access, the education of many non-technical users with respect to security if gaining in traction all the time. Many of the main social networks offer simple to enroll services such as OATH based OTP generators embedded within their apps (Facebook) or the sending of a OTP via text (Twitter).

Analysing requirements for MFA service selection will cover a range of different factors, including cost, usability and effective security. However, there are other considerations too—namely around when MFA should be triggered or used. It is likely that a universal rollout of MFA for every user, during every login event, from every device may not result in the most effective cost, user or security experience. It is important to consider applying the correct level of friction at the correct time–and that may mean applying MFA selectively, based on particular events, conditions or policy.

Scenarios driving requirements for MFA typically include:

- Login from a previously unknown device
- Access to a particular application
- Processing of a high risk event or transaction
- Login from a particular network/IP/domain/geofence boundary
- User event history
- Impossible travel test

The above events are typically going to be driven by basic risk analysis steps outlined in any corporate security objective the organisation building the CIAM solution should have.
"High risk events" are clearly going to be project and organisation specific, but typically cover items such as changes to billing, contact or postal addresses if used. Any event where high levels of monetary transactions are involved typically would trigger extra authentication steps too.

Other high risk events can be attached to behaviour–either wild changes in behaviour of the individual over a period of time, or changes for a single individual against a comparative peer group. If a user typically makes small purchases via the mobile app on their Android device on a weekend, but suddenly orders goods worth five times the previous 6 months purchases from a laptop device in an unusual location, that could seem like a fraudulent attack. In addition, if a group of users are deemed to be similar in composition–sex, age, location, income, social status–and one of those users performs an action not fitting to the peer group, that in turn could trigger an MFA barrier.

We will touch on future roadmapping a little later, but authentication is a constantly changing technological space and any requirements defined here, need to be thought about in the context of 12, 24 and 36 month cycles.

- What new authentication modalities are likely to be introduced in the next 24 months?
- What high risk functions will be introduced into the service in the next 24 months?
- Can the existing authentication components be swapped out in a modular fashion?

That last point is of vital importance. In the world of digital transformation which CIAM will help power, changes to the login process will have fundamental impacts on service use, usability and happiness. By being able to make rapid changes that reflect external technology, behaviour or market trends is essential to keeping pace with digital agility.

Many components in the CIAM service stack should be modular enough and loosely coupled to provide the ability for business as usual style changes to service and functionality. This applies increasingly to authentication based capabilities.

One last comment on authentication. Requirements analysis in this area should also look to capture the non-identity related services and pieces of data that are likely to need integrating. We touched on zero trust and CARTA in earlier chapters, and both concepts promote a high level of integration with regards to data such as device hygiene, threat intelligence and breached credentials. Deciding which services to integrate with will be determined by the general security and fraud posture of the organisation. Some basic integration concepts will be consistent however. Again, modular and standards based integration should be preferred, using standard developer friendly ideas such as simply to integrate SDKs with APIs based on REST and JSON. We will touch on these concepts in detail in chapter 7.

- ★ Provide a range of authentication options to cover user preference, device coverage and location
- ★ Authentication components should be modular and loosely coupled
- ★ Seek to integrate third party data sources for fraud, device management and threat intelligence

Authorization

Once a user has authenticated and the service "knows who

they are", the next part of the process requires understanding what they can do, and when. The process of authorization.

Unlike employee IAM where authorization is a large component of the overall service, CIAM authorization may again end up being shallow and broad–fewer complex entitlements and enforcement requirements, but across a large volume of users.

Authorization can come in many flavours. Implementation options have typically followed the RBAC (role based access control) and ABAC (attribute based access control) models in recent years. There are numerous other variants, most less popular and specialised such as task based access control, relationship based access control and capability based access control.

From a CIAM perspective, there are likely to be two main requirements to discuss: how access control decisions should be enforced and what mechanics for policy design and ruling should be used?

If we start with the enforcement point, that becomes easier if the project can describe what resources need protection. Will they be legacy applications built on Java or .NET frameworks, modern microservices and APIs or cloud and third party applications?

Protection

Protection typically comes in a few different flavours:

- Agents–small pieces of software sitting in front of the target application, typically at the HTTP/web container level
- Gateway–reverse proxy or network intercept gateway (software or hardware) that introspects and routes traffic to downstream APIs
- Native–applications perform the authorization internally using rules coded in software
- Callout–the API or application calls out to a central or distributed decision point with the subject (user), object (thing being protected) and action the user wants to perform and awaits a decision

In the microservices and API driven world, there are two slightly different protection models –one inline and one sidecar. The inline model is similar to a gateway–it will sit in front of an API (or APIs) and perform routing, throttling and some token introspection tasks. A side-car is slightly more focused–servicing only a single API and acts more like a response mechanism, outsourcing authorization decisioning away from the API or service. It is likely the side-car and inline mechanisms for microservices are more inclined to be more autonomous and distributed in their design and can make the majority of the enforcement decisions themselves, without having to callout to a centralised engine or third party system. This improves performance and allows for better scaling and tear down.

From a requirements perspective it is important to know what resources are being protected and the level of integration those resources are able to tolerate. Many of the above mechanisms promote the externalised view of enforcement, where the applications and APIs are relatively free from change–they continue to focus on the business service they operate, whilst outsourcing the authorization components to a dedicated function.

That model is typically a positive move for most application owners. However, be aware that requirements would need to be consistently defined regarding what the enforcement point does and what information it provides to the downstream system. It is typical that once the enforcement has taken place, that the downstream system being protected receives user and request information, such as userid's, device and transaction context and perhaps risk data too. How that gets presented (trusted header, JSON payload or other) and the specific attributes may differ from API to API so it is important to create a baseline of what attributes are to be offered and in what format.

Policy

Irregardless of whether a centralised or distributed decision point is being used, some sort of ruling or policy system is likely to be needed, that manages the relationship between the users and the underlying resources. Who can access what, when and under what context is a more typical question than authorization policy systems attempt to answer. Policy systems are generally made up of a few different components, namely the policy admin point where business or application owners can actually create the policies. They could be quite well decoupled from the more technical enforcement components, and aim to capture the underlying business context and tasks that need protecting. As the audience is more business orientated, usability and natural language processing for statements such as "can Sally update her postal address on a Sunday evening from an Android tablet" or "can the marketing system use Don's email address to promote a third party owned service we've just partnered with".

Many policy design and storage systems exist, both commercially or home grown but it's important to identify what is being protected and the impact of not protecting those systems correctly. What would be the cost of a data breach, misaligned access or continual access denials? Would it be a fine, end users calling the help desk or worse yet, end users moving to another service?

CIAM brings a set of new requirements around data protection, namely the inbound use of PII and third party sharing, as well as more the obvious aspects surrounding data breach protection regarding outbound access. Both the inbound–or ingress–processing of who can access what, as well the outbound–or egress–processing which may focus on redaction, tokenization or data attribute removal will all contribute to how policies should be designed.

★ Be in a position to understand what needs protecting and what those systems require from an information perspective
★ Policy design should help support business requirements surrounding roles, tasks, compliance and regulation
★ Focus on both the inbound and outbound processing of data to handle fine grained control of redaction and attribute removal

Scale & Capacity

One of the major differences between employee identity and consumer facing identity is that of scale. Scale in the form of capacity–so the ability to store records, profiles and data for millions of users–as well as the throughput capacity–logins per second for example. Both will be significantly higher than any system that is focused purely on internal or employee based users.

The difficulty with scale is estimation. With an employee

based system, vendors will typically ask a client "how many staff do you have in your HR system?", or perhaps "how many users will access the system from your federated partners?". Relatively closed questions that provide decent estimations of the future usage of the systems.

With a CIAM based application or service, asking "how many users will login?", the question is not quite as clear cut. As with the User Coverage section there is likely to be some well defined target audiences and usage patterns that will contribute to an underlying baseline of expected usage.

If engaging in commercial discussions with a provider, not only will those estimates need to be accurate, but they also help to hold a supplier to account, regarding can they be fulfilled with all the necessary service level agreements, thresholds and metrics. As the initial figures for user capacity may well be estimates, there are chances they could be 10%, 15% or 25% below or above reality. If so, that needs to be reflected in any commercial agreements. If your service attracts 25% less registrations than expected, can a refund or deferred payment be arranged? If the reverse and 25% higher numbers are experienced, can the service provider respond to such changes in a timely manner without impacting the service or perhaps imposing a fine or penalty?

If designing homegrown parts of the solution, that level of elasticity (for both expansion and retraction) would be key to not only for cost effective maintenance, but also operational support and responsiveness too.

Whilst the estimation process is difficult, it is often key to understanding what is likely to introduce spike events. These are likely to be external triggers that cause significant changes to your target user community behaviour. Are there certain marketing events, promotions or partnerships that may have real positive shifts in attention and registration? Are there situations which result in peak usage, followed by long lags of inertia or "down time" such as during competitions or sporting events?

By identifying those external triggers, the impact and predictability may become more stable.

★ Try and identify best estimate high water marks for throughput and storage
★ Identify likely external factors that influence user behaviour and user expectation
★ External supplier agreements should be flexible enough to allow for below and above estimate reality that doesn't result in penalties or delay

Future Roadmap

Any engaged supplier or vendor is likely to have a roadmap of expected future capabilities. Sometimes this is a public document or web page, other times a more confidential document available via a signed non-disclosure agreement. Those roadmaps are useful to help understand a supplier's "north star" or compass regarding their strategy and the factors that are influencing their decision making. They can be useful documents to help decide if a supplier is a good long term fit.

Conversely, it is important to develop a roadmap for the future required capabilities the CIAM platform may require or encounter as it develops. This helps to focus the CIAM service as a product in its own right–and not a finite set of services with a limited implementation lifecycle. CIAM is a fundamental part of the organisation's transformation and a key middleware component that integrates and touches lots of different systems. It is important to treat it as a "living service", that will continue to evolve, grow and alter as the user, application and market trends change too.

By treating the service as a product, allows standard product management concepts to be adopted such as future requirements analysis, a roadmap of new components and a set of teams and resources that provide continual redesign and iteration.

Many complex middleware projects historically, often had a "launch" date, followed by migration into standard operating models of support. The teams as part of that standard operating model, would be focused on day to day operations, not on evolution and feature iteration.
The end result was often a "big bang" style of delivery and analysis, where a "develop and deploy" pattern emerged, followed by a period of between 3 to 5 years of standard operating support and incremental updates.

This cycle would continue, where another period of analysis would be followed by a period of sustaining support and another period of analysis, design and new service introduction.

Digital transformation is more about focusing on solving the unknown problem of market change, adoption and new service introduction. Performing isolated periods of analysis, launch and support can produce a service that rapidly becomes outdated and unable to evolve to external requirements.

Having a relatively product focused approach to CIAM functionality allows organisations to move away from the "big bang" and apply a continually iterative approach to service delivery.

A part of that process is the building of a roadmap. Roadmaps can serve several purposes, from outbound and internal messaging, through to helping decide and describe a priority process for bugs and enhancements. A roadmap should also help to clearly articulate what the service "will not" do or deliver. The not todo, is equally important as the todo and can act as a catalyst for strategic discussion for where the service is heading.

From a requirements perspective, it is important to be able to *empathise* and then *synthesise* user requirements across a range of the different stakeholders discussed in *chapter 5.*

What political, economic, social and technological (PEST)

challenges will they be facing over a 24-36 month period? Why are those challenges important? What is the impact if those challenges are not solved? What is the economic cost of inaction versus implementation?

Some typical areas of focus should be on changes to user coverage, authentication options, device integrations and resource protection.

- ★ Continually iterate with the CIAM stakeholder teams to identify future patterns of demand for functional and non-functional requirements
- ★ Leverage a PEST model or an external set of factors that influence decision making
- ★ Build roadmaps for internal and external communities that communicate the vision, in order to trigger responses and capture feedback

Summary

This chapter was focused on some of the basic building blocks that help to develop knowledge surrounding some of the more specific requirements and their impact on the service design.

CIAM will touch and integrate upon many roles and business functions. Requirements gathering should not be done in isolation from the business requirements, but also needs to focus on the lower level functional aspects that will make the service successful.

Asking questions is a simple and powerful way of capturing

requirements for a service, as is observing user and system behaviour. The results of that process should provide a basis for continuous and iterative feedback to the various solution owners

Our next chapter will alter our direction a little and provide some high level technical descriptions of some of the key pieces of functionality, libraries and standards that may be used during solution implementation.

CHAPTER 7

Implementer Toolbox

This chapter will focus upon providing a baseline level of understanding of the key standards, libraries and concepts that are likely to feature within a CIAM solution. The idea is not to provide a full and detailed architecture, but more the skills needed to listen, understand and communicate with subject matter experts in a range of different technical areas. The information will be bite size and pragmatic and will not assume any prior knowledge on each of the sections we will cover.

Whilst many readers may not be implementers or come from a technical background, the chapter is concise and I advise reading through it anyway, in order to at least understand some of the challenges that colleagues and solution owners may face and some of the terminology they may use.

Cryptography Crash Course

I want to start with an area that often ignites either detailed passionate conversations on the future of security, privacy and national safety, right through to those heading in every other direction to avoid what is seen as an abstract, obtuse and difficult to understand topic. The fact remains, cryptography powers many technologies, both identity and security related.

We start with cryptography, firstly as it underpins many of the remaining standards and topics in this chapter and secondly to overcome some of the misconceptions that it can be difficult to understand.

Cryptography can be used in lots of different ways to provide a multitude of different services and functions. The main one is that of upholding confidentiality with regards to sensitive data. That data could be top secret battle plans, someone's medical test results or a competitor's price list. Many pieces of data require elements of confidentiality - and applying restrictions on who can access something. Of course, cryptography is not the only tool required to make this possible. Authentication, authorization, access control systems and so on, all play an important part.

If cryptography were a medicine, it could be seen as the antibiotic within the doctor's kit bag - a useful and essential tool, perhaps over used and often seen as the magic bullet. Cryptography alone will not provide the security many think and an end to end set of components and services are required to make it successful.

Let us start by adding a glossary, in order to become familiar with some of the key terms often used when describing cryptography.

Figure 7.1 Cryptography shortened glossary

Term/Acronym	Description
Cryptography	Coming from the Ancient Greek word of 'kryptos' meaning hidden or secret. The practice of securing communications from adversaries, but often now applied to static data too.
Cryptanalysis	Analysing an information system to understand hidden or unseen aspects. Often used to describe the process of finding secret keys used in cryptography.
Ciphertext	The output of a cryptosystem that is unintelligible to the human eye. Often referred to as being "scrambled".
Cryptosystem	The combination of one of more primitive building blocks that form an algorithm that is used to perform cryptographic operations such as encryption or decryption.
Primitive	Most basic building mathematical block. Performs a very succinct function and needs to be highly reliable and repeatable.
Plaintext/Cleartext	The original human readable message before it enters the

	cryptosystem. Typically what an adversary would want to see or steal.
Secret Key	A set of characters that are used as an ingredient into the cryptosystem to help create the final output. Is typically not public and is kept secure.
Random Generator	A routine that is used to generate random output that is used as an ingredient either to create secret keys or used with them. True randomness tends to come from natural sources and is transformed into a digital medium.
Pseudo Random Generator	As true random generators are difficult to implement, substitutes are used which are "pseudo" random - they look random, but may create repeatable patterns.

Cryptography clearly isn't useful just to CIAM, but it might help to imagine where it can play a part, before we can break down some of those journeys into their respective parts. If we imagine a new user registering for a CIAM service, there are some basic functions where cryptography has a role to play. Firstly the link between the user's device and the web application they're accessing - this should be over an encrypted link (aka the HTTPS and padlock in the browser's address bar, instead of just HTTP). The process to make this work is essentially using a protocol called Transport Layer Security (TLS). Once that the registration payload arrives at the destination web site, the user profile will need storing within a database or directory. The immediate thought would be to securely store the user's password. This would be done using a hashing algorithm - which stores the password in a way that cannot be reversed back into its plaintext form.

Figure 7.2 CIAM example uses of cryptography during user registration

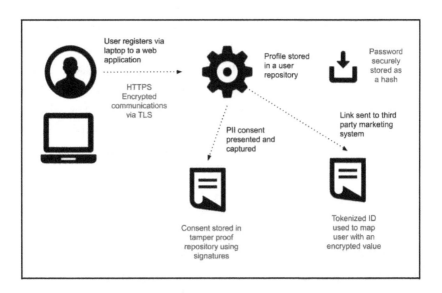

What about other pieces of data that the CIAM service would start to capture and process? There are likely to be consent capture dialogues to manage, where explicit actions surrounding PII processing would need actioning. It is likely that once consent has been given, the details surrounding that consent will be stored in a way that can't be tampered or altered. Cryptography could be used for that too, perhaps by creating digital signatures on entries to validate the time, date and individual who issued consent.

Other potential uses of cryptography, could include how data is linked and processed by integrated third parties. Marketing systems may well need to track user interactions, but equally they may need to handle such processing in a way that anonymises the true identity of the end user. Concepts such as tokenization may come into play here, with real identifiers being replaced by references, perhaps based on an encrypted value.

As we can see, even in such a simple user flow, cryptography rears its head on several occasions, even without complexity or customisation. Many of the above concepts would leverage standard algorithms, likely supported by existing libraries and implementations.

Let us take some of the main concepts and add a bit of detail.

Encryption

Encryption is the focus on taking a piece of plaintext and converting it into ciphertext - and essentially back again. Being able to encrypt something, typically requires that it can be decrypted and returned to its original state. The main driver for this process, was the passing of messages from one party to the other - across a typically untrusted channel. Perhaps a set of horse drawn messengers travelling through the lawless mountain trails of the 17th century, right through to the untrusted set of network nodes on the Internet of today.

The entire process will include several different components, but for simplicity we can break that down into an encryption function, a secret key, the plaintext message and a decryption function.

The two parties involved in the exchange, agree on the encryption and decryption functions. The other piece of information the sender and receiver need to agree upon is the secret key used to encrypt the message. If the receiver wants to be able to decrypt the message and return it back to the original, they too will also need that secret key. This is a non-trivial task. How do you get a secret key from one party to the other, without the adversary stealing the key and accessing the message? If we had a secure way of doing that, we probably wouldn't need to encrypt the message in the first place! There are several ways this can be achieved however.

Either using some powerful mathematical concepts where two parties can generate a secret number without actually sharing that number publicly, or by using a secondary encryption system based on different keys that are used to just encrypt the secret used for encrypting the messages. The details of which are a little beyond the scope of this chapter however.

Symmetric Key Encryption

A popular type of data encryption process is that of symmetric encryption. Here the term symmetric refers to the fact that the secret key is used by both the encrypting *and* decrypting functions. Some examples of symmetric ciphers include DES (data encryption standard) and AES (advanced encryption standard).

Block Ciphers

Symmetric encryption can be broken down into two areas: block ciphers and stream ciphers. Block ciphers, as the name indicates, break down the plaintext input, into nice repeating sized chunks, called "blocks". The encryption function then works on encrypting each block one at a time until all the plaintext has been converted into ciphertext. One other term that you may hear when it comes to block ciphers, is that of padding. Clearly if the size of the plaintext doesn't neatly break down into a set of blocks, you may need to "pad out" the message with extra data to make it fit. This is known as padding and there are secure ways of doing this that don't expose details of the underlying message.

Stream Ciphers

In addition to block ciphers, symmetric encryption can utilise stream ciphers. They work not on individual blocks of the plaintext, but typically one bit at a time, in a continual stream, until all bits of the plaintext are encrypted. The original plaintext message is added together to a "key stream" - which is essentially a random looking set of 1's and 0's that is derived from a secret key. Stream ciphers are typically very fast and simple to implement within hardware.

Asymmetric Encryption

Whilst symmetric encryption relies on both the receiver and sender to be in possession of the same secret key, another concept called asymmetric encryption, based on public key cryptography, doesn't have such a requirement. Asymmetric encryption involves two keys typically known as a public key and a private key. The private one, is kept private, but the public one is and should be made available to other parties. The keys are related and can be mathematically proven to originate from the same generation process.

This asymmetry can create some interesting properties. Firstly, encryption with a public key, can allow for the decryption with the corresponding private key. In the classic "Alice wants to share a message with Bob" scenario, both Alice and Bob generate their own public and private key pairs: $Alice_{Private}$ and $Alice_{Public}$ and $Bob_{Private}$ and Bob_{Public}.

If Bob wants to send a secure message to Alice, he would encrypt it using the $Alice_{Public}$ key. The only person who can decrypt that message is Alice as she has the corresponding Alice$_{Private}$ key - hopefully she has kept that key secure. If Alice wants to send a response back to Bob, she would encrypt her message using Bob$_{Public}$ - which only Bob with his Bob$_{Private}$ key could decrypt.

Asymmetric cryptosystems were developed in the 1970s and made commercially viable by Ron Rivest, Adi Shamir and Leonard Adleman - namely the RSA public key cryptosystem.

So if asymmetric encryption solves the issue regarding the sharing of secret keys, why is symmetric encryption used at all?

Well typically symmetric encryption and decryption processes are much faster than asymmetric ones. What typically occurs in real world deployments, is some sort of hybrid implementation, where the symmetric key used for encrypting the actual plaintext messages, is encrypted using the asymmetric cryptosystem.

Hashing

Another related cryptographic term to be aware of, is that of hashing. Whilst encryption is typically a two way process (with a corresponding reversible decryption process) hashing is focused on being one way. That is, it is not reversible. Think of hashing being synonymous with dropping a glass mirror on to a concrete floor. Not only is that quite a difficult (aka virtually impossible) task to reverse and end up with the mirror back in pristine condition, but also very difficult to replicate. If you dropped two near identical mirrors at the same time, you will get two very different patterns of broken glass. The same should be true of hashing.

The simplified view of the hash process is essentially a function that takes the plaintext human readable data and produces a fixed length output, that looks like an entirely different scrambled string. The scrambled output should bear no resemblance to the plaintext input and there should be no way of being able to reverse the function. The hash function does not require the need for a secret key either. The algorithm can operate without the need for a key and is merely a standalone function. A common hashing algorithm is SHA256, standing for the secure hashing algorithm 256 bits edition. The 256 bits refers to the length of the output. For example:

The text "This is my password" run through the SHA256 algorithm results in:

```
Cac2b524c0e488dcace6618a6899a4736866cc3bf41b6fc
bf4e56e558be75cfa
```

The text "This is my 2nd password" run through the SHA256 algorithm results in:

```
7e052565361cff0921a87ae750a40e7ee365d94392af4b2
43f6e4edf6b15a1ea
```

Note the input was only a slightly bit different, but the output hash is entirely different - however exactly the same length - 256bits.

Hashes are used for many things, but password storage is the most typical in a CIAM deployment architecture.

Another term to be aware of when it comes to hashing, is that of a "salt". When using hashes for password storage, two different users may inadvertently choose the same password. As a result the hashes for these users will be the same. In order to avoid disclosing this information to an adversary, a salt is added to the hashing process. This salt is an additional string to help add variety to the hash output. Ideally the salt should be unique per hash run through.

Signatures

A close relative to hashing, is that of digital signatures. In the physical world, we use signatures to provide confirmation and assurance regarding authenticity of payment, acceptance of terms or other binding legal agreements. How can we replicate that process in the digital world? We would need characteristics that would make a digital signature easy to create, difficult to forge and be somehow tied to the content that is being signed. A digital signature should not be lifted from one document and applied to another for example.

Digital signatures look to solve two problems: one, that the message came from the correct sender (proving authentication) and two that the message hasn't been changed on route to the receiver (providing integrity).

If Alice wants to send her message to Bob, and Bob wants evidence that Alice did in fact send it, both hashing and an asymmetric cryptographic system could be used. A hash of the message being sent is created, which in turn is signed (maybe along with a timestamp) using Alice's private key. Don't forget, the private key should be kept private at all times, so only Alice can perform this operation. Bob can use Alice's public key to verify the signature to confirm it was Alice that sent the message. This non-repudiation aspect (removing the ability for someone to deny they performed an action) is a powerful tool in the legal processing of events. Assuming Alice has kept her private key private, she cannot claim someone else sent the message (or approved a request) on her behalf.

Signatures could be a useful tool when it comes to consent management in the CIAM space. With PII management and healthcare data sharing and control, digital signatures provide a way of verifying actions that require approvals and agreements in a digital landscape.

Message Authentication Codes

Message Authentication Codes or MACs, are a cousin to digital signature schemes, except they rely on symmetric keys, not asymmetric ones. In this case the key used to create a tag on a particular piece of data, is also the same key used in the verification of the tag.

Whilst this is very useful (and fast), it also removes the

ability to perform full non-repudiation to third parties, as both the sender and receiver have the same key. The receiver, if malicious, could craft a message claiming it was from the sender. MACs are likely to be used in communications systems more than individual to individual service validation.

This was a very high level introduction to some rudimentary cryptography concepts. For those wishing to delve a little deeper, a very accessible book on the topic is "Everyday Cryptography" by Keith Martin[129].

The rest of this chapter will take a pragmatic look at some implementation building blocks used in CIAM platforms. Each section will take a glossary, example and key terms approach in order to provide the reader with a set of baseline principles.

APIs, REST and JSON

APIs

Stands for: Application Programming Interface

Used for: Abstracting the underlying function of a system by the means of a well described set of function entry points and data flows.

Background: APIs provide the interface into the inner workings of a particular function or service. The API is the

---

129https://www.isg.rhul.ac.uk/~martin/

entry point and will describe how other systems or clients can trigger an event, retrieve or create data and under what particular circumstances.

APIs help to break functional logic down into small bite size chunks. Each API is likely to be dependent on other APIs but in a loosely coupled way. This loose coupling allows for changes to be made to one API function, without impacting another. This decoupling along with well described APIs allows for functions to be written in different languages and by different teams.

The API descriptions can be used by different application owners, who are developing client applications or complementary functions. When combined this API integration pattern can deliver highly complex functionality.

REST

Stands for: Representational State Transfer.

Used for: A set of constraints used to describe the building blocks of web service APIs

Background: APIs used to power web services, are often also based on REST concepts. REST focuses on using HTTP verbs such as GET, POST, DELETE, PUT and PATCH. GET is used to read, POST for creating, DELETE for deleting (!), PUT for updating entire records and PATCH for updating specific attributes. Those verbs function against well described resources, or URIs (universal resource identifiers).

There are several well described principles REST APIs work towards, namely being stateless (each request is separate and unlinked), are loosely coupled and portable with a level of simplicity.

JSON

Stands for: JavaScript Object Notation.

Used for: A standardised data format, used to serialise data, so it can be stored and transported by different systems.

Background: JSON is a lightweight and language independent data format, used in conjunction with REST based APIs to return data payloads to calling clients and applications. The format is human readable and is formed of various different "key/value" pairs. A key being an attribute name, the value being its value. The entire payload is encapsulated in opening and closing curly brackets. Attribute types include string, boolean (true/false), array (ordered list of more than one value) or another object - often referred to as nested JSON.

Libraries exist in all of the major programming languages and are well understood amongst the developer community.
Entries are comma separated, with indentation for

readability. Associated schema objects are also used, which describe explicitly what each object should contain, what the attribute type each value is expected to have and so on.

An example JSON object to present a user identity could be the following:

```
{
    "firstName": "John",
    "lastName": "Smith",
    "email": "john.smith@domain.com",
    "emailVerified": true,
    "phoneNumbers": [
        {
            "type": "home",
            "number": "212 555-1234"
        },
        {
            "type": "office",
            "number": "646 555-4567"
        }
    ]
}
```

An older data format that was prevalent before JSON was XML.

OAuth2

Stands for: Open Authorization mk2.

Used for: Standards based authorization interactions in the modern web.

Background: A standard for Internet authorization, developed and released by the Internet Engineering Task For (IETF) and ratified in October 2012 under the name of RFC6749[130]. OAuth2 has no interoperability with it's cousin OAuth1[131] - of which very few implementations exist.

OAuth2 is focused on removing the anti-pattern of password sharing from the modern web, by allowing third party access to an HTTP based resource or application, which is acting on behalf of a resource owner who has given consent. Instead of these third parties having to know the resource owners password, they receive a time based and scoped access token.

This access token is shown to an API or resource server in order to retrieve data or perform an action. The resource owner (a real user entity) approves a consent flow allowing the application access. The resource owner can of course, revoke access when necessary. A concept of an authorization server or service exists, which issues (and revokes) the necessary access tokens. The third party never receives any password or credentials for the end user.

The access token typically has an exp attribute (referring to the expiry time), a sub attribute (referring to the subject identifier the token belongs to) and an scp attribute (or scopes attribute). The scopes refer to the permissions or entitlements the access token has acquired. An example

130https://tools.ietf.org/html/rfc6749
131https://tools.ietf.org/html/rfc5849

scope could be READ_API or perhaps in the case of Facebook Graph API[132] permissions "email" - which refers to the access token being able to read a user's Facebook registered email address.

If you wanted to allow a third party gaming application to access your Facebook profile and post on your activity wall, you would very likely be using OAuth2 under the hood to allow the interaction to take place.

OAuth2 MTLS

Stands for: OAuth2 Mutual Transport Layer Security.

Used for: Authenticating client applications to an OAuth2 authorization service.

Background: When an application wishes to interact with an OAuth2 authorization service, the client application typically needs to authenticate itself. There are some cases (where the client is known as a public client) where that authentication process may not take place, but for "confidential" clients, the application needs to provide a clientId and secret. Each application will have a unique clientId and secret, used to identify and authenticate themselves. However, as with users, passwords are not seen as the most secure way of authenticating something. To increase application authentication assurance OAuth2 MTLS was introduced. This follows another IETF standard namely called RFC8705[133].

132https://developers.facebook.com/docs/facebook-login/permissions/overview
133https://tools.ietf.org/html/rfc8705

MTLS uses asymmetric cryptography with public and private key pairs generated and assigned to each client application. Instead of providing a secret (or password) during application to authorization server attachment, a set of cryptographic exchanges will take place, using the common place TLS infrastructure found in many web application containers and gateways. The "mutual" aspect provides assurance that not only is the server side connection authenticated, but also the client application side too, providing a higher level of assurance.

Another aspect of MTLS with OAuth2, is that tokens that are issued using this method, can also be "certificate bound" - meaning that they contain information relating to the client's certificate used during the MTLS authentication. This extra information can allow resource servers who receive the access token during an access request, to perform a challenge/response validation check, to verify if the requester using the access token does indeed have access to the corresponding private key. This provides extra layers of security to reduce the impact of token theft.

OAuth2 MTLS is common in CIAM ecosystems where a high level of assurance is necessary, such as financial services and retail banking.

OAuth2 PKCE
Stands for: OAuth2 Proof Key Code Exchange.

Used for: To reduce the impact from theft of the authorization code used to request access tokens.

Background: Client applications in the OAuth2 paradigm, request access tokens from the OAuth2 authorization service. The client application, then uses that access token to request access to data or functions at the resource server. There are a couple of ways that the client can request an access token, but the most common (and secure way according to the OAuth2 Best Current Practice[134]) is to use something called the authorization code grant. During this flow, upon the completion of a request to the authorization service to authenticate the user, the authorization service sends back an authorization code. This code is typically opaque to the client - that is it is entirely reference based and doesn't leak any information.

The client uses this authorization code to request an access token from the authorization server. With the access token, the client can perform access requests to the resource server.

There is an issue however, that could result in the authorization code being stolen by a malicious app residing on the same device as the legitimate one. The PKCE process seeks to reduce the impact of such a theft. PKCE is defined by another IETF standard called RFC7636[135]. Essentially during this process, the client application sends an authorization code request along with a hash of a secret

134https://tools.ietf.org/html/draft-ietf-oauth-security-topics-16
135https://tools.ietf.org/html/rfc7636

value. The authorization service stores this hash and sends back the authorization code. When the client application comes to exchange the authorization code for an access token, it also sends a long the original secret value, which the authorization uses to compare to the hashed version that was stored from the first request. If they match a token is issued.

PKCE is the recommended process for public clients that typically exist in mobile applications.

OAuth2 Device Grant

Stands for: Whilst not an acronym, it refers to the OAuth2 Device Authorization Grant RFC8628[136]

Used For: When the client application in an OAuth2 ecosystem, is operating on a smart IoT related device, that isn't capable of having full user interface or keyboard interactions.

Background: Over the last 5 years, IoT devices have emerged as standard integrating components of a CIAM ecosystem. From smart TV's and sports equipment to fitness and medical wearables, these IoT devices have considerable power and can represent a user to any protected API or downstream system. Instead of the many custom and proprietary ways of integrating these devices, the OAuth2 ecosystem has developed a specific profile just for such interactions.

136https://tools.ietf.org/html/rfc8628

The Device Authorization Grant, essentially allows the device to receive an access token bearer payload, that represents a paired user. The user provides consent for the device on the back of an out of band authentication dance that occurs on a laptop or smartphone - essentially a secondary device that has enough user interface and keyboard capabilities to allow a login and entry of a pairing code.

The pairing code is sent to the device from a pre-registered authorization service, after the user has triggered a pairing event on the device. The user takes the pairing code (or perhaps scans it via a QR code) and enters it on a separate page on the authorization service. Once paired, the authorization service sends back an access token with limited scopes to the smart device.

The smart device then acts like any other application and interacts with APIs and applications on the user's behalf. The device has access until the access (or refresh) tokens expire, or until the user manually revokes the access, requiring a new pairing event.

UMA

Stands for: User Managed Access.

Used for: A protocol that sits atop of OAuth2, that provides user centric authorization control.

Background: UMA is another standard, this time managed

by the Kantara Initiative[137]. UMA is broken down into two parts - the UMA Grant and the UMA Federated Authorization Recommendations. The main premise is that UMA provides a framework for an end user to create authorization rules that allow access to the user's data or managed applications.

In a typical authorization landscape, control is managed via IT administrators or application owners. In the modern web, with CIAM at its foundation, end user data control is passed across to the actual data owner - in this case the end user themselves.

Through a complex framework of interactions, the end user is able to create rules on an authorization service either at run time, or in advance to share individual pieces of data or perhaps long time access to a particular data function or service, to other individuals.

A classic example is the sharing of healthcare data to trusted third parties within a healthcare ecosystem. Those parties could include healthcare practitioners, insurers or online services. The data owner - the end user - is put front and centre in control of who can access that data and when.

As the flows sit on top of OAuth2 and can therefore take advantage of concepts such as REST and JSON based standards integration, MTLS, PKCE and so on.

137https://kantarainitiative.org/confluence/display/uma/Home

OIDC

Stands for: OpenID Connect.

Used for: An authentication layer that sits atop of OAuth2. A standard developed by the OpenID Foundation[138].

Background: Whilst OAuth2 is focused on authorization, OIDC is focused upon authentication. It again utilises the foundation provided by OAuth2, which is REST, JSON and API based. OIDC aims to provide more assurances around the subject (or user) involved in the authorization process. It does this via the introduction of another token - this time the id token. This id token, as the name suggests, is focused upon providing information relating to the identity. The format of this token is a JWT - or JSON Web Token and pronounced as "jot".

This token is a cryptographically signed (and sometimes encrypted) JSON object that contains multiple attributes related to the user's identity. These attributes are known as "claims". There are a number of standard claims within the official spec, such as given_name, family_name, email, email_verified and so on. Other claims of course can be added to the token as necessary, which may help downstream systems make more informed decisions with regards to the access control.

Different client applications can request specific claims when they request a token, allowing quite fine grained and service specific tokens. Claims could also come from

138https://openid.net/specs/openid-connect-core-1_0.html

differing systems, in the form of aggregated claims (gathering information from other sources) and distributed claims (meaning the client can collect additional information).

OIDC is equivalent in many respects to a modern day SAML. SAML (or security assertion markup language) is an older protocol based on XML, that was popular during the 2000s and was the de facto way of providing cross-party federation information in the form of assertions.

From a CIAM perspective, whilst sometimes used in systems that help to administer and power the CIAM platform, from an inbound user perspective SAML is seen less.

JWT

Stands for: JSON Web Token, and pronounced "jot".

Used for: A standard way of providing cryptographic signing (and sometimes encryption) of JSON objects for authenticity. Often seen as a format for OAuth2 access tokens and OIDC id tokens.

Background: JWT tokens are commonly found in the REST/JSON/API world and certainly where OAuth2 access tokens are used. The OAuth2 spec does not explicitly describe the token format of access tokens and the two main token models typically fall into either being "reference" tokens or "stateless" tokens.

A reference approach is where the token that is sent back from the authorization service is typically an opaque string, resembling a globally unique identifier such as 4h3399-2sdcaff-1123da. The client and resource server gain no information directly from the token and require the use of "introspection" endpoints from the issuing authorization service to be able to validate and retrieve the token contents.

A stateless approach, refers to the authorization service issuing the token material as a JWT. This JWT is typically human readable - albeit in some instances the token could be encrypted. If not encrypted, the format resembles that of a JSON object, but with some additional information - namely a "header" and "signature". The signature is a cryptographically generated component that uses standard symmetric key message authentication code or asymmetric key signature algorithms and is appended to the end of the JSON object. The header contains some meta information regarding how the signature was generated.

The entire payload is then encoded, using something called base64. Base64 encoding essentially allows the token to be passed around the web infrastructure without certain characters within the token being dropped or erroneously constructed. A JWT will look something like the following:

eyJhbGciOiJIUzI1NiIsInR5cCI6IkpXVCJ9.eyJzdWIiOi
IxMjM0NTY3ODkwIiwibmFtZSI6IkpvaG4gRG9lIiwiaWF0I
joxNTE2MjM5MDIyfQ.SflKxwRJSMeKKF2QT4fwpMeJf36PO

```
k6yJV_adQssw5c
```

For the keen eyed, that weird string, is "dot delimited" and prefixed "ey". The header, payload and signature components are separated by "dots". The "ey" is indicating the start of a curly bracket "{" in base64.

All in, the JWT becomes a self contained token, that can be validated by resource servers that have access to the necessary symmetric signing key, or asymmetric public key. This can be a useful property, as having to always call back to the authorization server to validate a token could encounter network latency and access delays.

However, one issue that can occur with JWTs is the inability to revoke a token before it's natural exp (or expiry) time has occurred. For example, say a JWT based access token was issued with read access to an API. The token has an exp of 2 hours - but 15 minutes after the token was issued, the authorization service receives an alert saying that the token needs invalidating as it has fallen into the hands of a malicious actor.

How can the token be invalidated if the resource server does not make a call back to the authorization service to validate? Essentially it can't. Technically there are several ways to solve the problem - perhaps sending an id of the issued token to the resource service via a push or web sockets notification. It is worth noting the concept however.

There are some useful tools available for constructing and introspecting JWTs - namely JWT.io[139] (developed by Auth0) and CyberChef[140] (an open source tool created by the UK's GCHQ for data and crypto manipulation).

FIDO & FIDO2/WebAuthn

FIDO

Stands for: Fast Identity Online.

Used for: Cryptographic based authentication protocol, used either as a second factor or potentially as a password replacement.

Background: FIDO is a standard that evolved out of the FIDO Alliance[141] - an open industry association that counts organisations such as Amazon, Apple, Google and RSA as members. They promote the use of public key cryptography as a way of securely authenticating people and things. There are essentially two dances: one to register to a service that supports FIDO and one to login or authenticate.

During the registration process a FIDO enabled website triggers a user's FIDO supported device to generate a new cryptographically secure key pair. The public key of that pair, is sent to the website along with other standard user profile details.

139https://jwt.io/
140https://gchq.github.io/CyberChef/
141https://fidoalliance.org/

Upon authentication back to the website or application the website triggers a challenge that is sent to the user's previously registered device. This challenge demands the device to prove possession of the corresponding private key by signing the challenge and sending it back to the website. The originating service can verify the challenge, by using the previously registered public key.

The private key on the device is "unlocked" to perform the challenge response, by means of a local authentication event - typically a user entering a PIN, or perhaps a biometric fingerprint scan. This essentially decouples the authentication processes away from the protected website or application.

No passwords or credentials travel over the network, which is typically seen as being insecure. The FIDO Alliance provides a nice website[142] describing the process in more detail.
Some other key terms that you may hear when FIDO is mentioned, is UAF and U2F. UAF stands for Universal Authentication Framework whilst U2F refers to Universal Second Factor.

The FIDO Alliance provides a catalog of certified components - both hardware devices and server side software that has gone through the official assessment process.

142https://fidoalliance.org/how-fido-works/

FIDO2 / WebAuthn

Stands for: Fast Identity Online mk2 and Web Authentication.

Used for: A second iteration of FIDO, that decouples some of the protocol components into a web based API accessible via modern browsers and the CTAP protocol for communicating to hardware devices.

Background: FIDO2 essentially over arches two components. The WebAuthn[143] protocol released by the W3C and the CTAP[144] protocol (client to authenticator protocol) managed by the FIDO Alliance. The aim of decoupling the protocols was a plan to increase adoption by driving cryptographic passwordless authentication to the modern web.

WebAuthn leverages a new API that is accessible via existing browser technology. Most modern browsers such as Microsoft Edge, Google Chrome and Mozilla Firefox support its implementation.

CTAP provides a set of lower level APIs that allow the browser to interact with hardware such as portable USB, Bluetooth or NFC security keys. These portable devices generate the asymmetric keys and respond to the challenges generated and handled by the WebAuthn API.

FIDO2 aims to solve the passwordless approach to login,

143https://www.w3.org/TR/webauthn/
144https://fidoalliance.org/specs/fido-v2.0-ps-20190130/fido-client-to-authenticator-protocol-v2.0-ps-20190130.pdf

using securely derived cryptographic credentials. Each website that is registered against using FIDO2, has its own key pair, resulting in a distributed pattern of security, where the unlikely breaching of a single private key, impacts only a single registered service.

FIDO2 also supports a new concept of "usernameless". This concept, applicable only to supported hardware, allows a user identifier to be stored alongside the generated key pair in order to remove the need to provide a username during the authentication dance.

SCIM

Stands for: System for Cross Domain Identity Management.

Used for: SCIM is focused on the life cycle management of user identities within cloud systems, by providing a REST/JSON API and associated schema that describes how to manage identity objects.

Background: IETF standards RFC7642, RFC7643 and RFC7644 ratified in September 2015, make up the SCIM[145] foundation. SCIM is concerned with how identity objects are created and essentially managed within cloud systems and resources. Think of SCIM as the layer that standardises the creation process, by allowing client applications and storage systems to agree upon the structure of identity data. The standard focuses upon the

145http://www.simplecloud.info/#Specification

main building blocks for identity data - users, groups and enterprise users as a specific sub category of user.

The schema definition is based on JSON, with an associated HTTP verb attachment for GET, POST, DELETE etc. SCIM also provides guidance around how SCIM services can be discovered using API discovery endpoints.

The specifications are broken down to support the base description (RFC7642), the protocol flow between clients and applications (RFC7643) and the schema definitions (RFC7644).

Support for the standard will follow either a client or server side model - with the client generating requests and the server providing an inbound API to accept identity data to an agreed up schema and protocol flow. The SCIM website provides a list of supported services in a plan to improve interoperability. The current version is 2.0. A 1.0 and 1.1 version exist, but adoption is likely low.

LDAP

Stands for: Lightweight Directory Access Protocol.

Used for: The directory storage of user (and sometimes device) data in a hierarchical way with a standardized set of protocols for access, storage and replication.

Background: LDAP has a long history in the Internet's

foundation. The most recent version, is v3, standardized in RFC4511[146]. The initial design for LDAP however, emerged in the 1990s, primarily within the telecommunications sector and the x500 set of standards. X500 is a large set of components focused on describing a DAP (directory access protocol), DSP (directory system protocol), DISP (directory information shadowing protocol) and DOP (directory object protocol). Another acronym of interest is DIT - the directory information tree, which is the hierarchical structuring of data into various branches.

LDAP is really a stripped down version of some of the concepts described in the x500 DAP. Whilst perhaps not the most cutting edge of technology, it provides a hugely important role in many internal and external facing identity platforms. Why? Because it provides the main foundation for the storage or large scale user data. Microsoft Active Directory (and Azure Active Directory) are based on LDAP.

Large scale user storage requires several basic properties. The ability to store large volumes. The ability to rapidly read back those entries. And the ability to replicate that data to different offices, sites and geographies at high speed, for fault tolerance and availability.

The schema description for LDAP results in entries based on their position within the DIT. For example, an entry for user called John Doe, may look like the following:

```
cn=john doe,ou=people,dc=uk,dc=acme,dc=org
```

146https://tools.ietf.org/html/rfc4511

The "cn" refers to the entry's common name the "ou" the organisational unit, the "dc" referring to the domain component.

LDAP based systems are often compared to relational databases for the storage of user data. Whilst many databases are capable of storing such data, LDAP based services typically focus solely on the storage of entities that require high throughput and high scale authentication - like user and device identities.

Summary

This chapter provided a high level look at some of the key standards and technical components that are likely to appear in large scale CIAM platforms. Whilst not exhaustive, it should provide a set of foundational concepts. Primarily, that standards are essential. Standards are available at all parts of the CIAM lifecycle from identity data storage and schematics, through to access, authentication and authorization.

Whilst the integration of these components is common and expected, the desire to "roll your own" should be low.

Many standards may seem complicated at first, but have the huge advantage of being peer reviewed and implemented in many other systems. This not only provides stability in design, but also accelerates interoperability.

CHAPTER 8

Vendor Selection Support

This chapter will focus upon providing some guidance around working with and selecting a trusted supplier or vendor for a CIAM platform. Selecting technology providers can be time consuming, complex and obtuse, due to a considerable information imbalance for both parties.

The supplier will be focused on promoting their key competencies and will clearly not be experts in understanding how a prospective client organisation works or operates. A buyer can find marketing, messaging and outbound descriptions of a supplier too coarse grained and lacking in real business value mapping.

Vendor Selection Process

A vendor selection process will often vary for each buyer. Factors such as industry vertical, regulatory constraints and being in the public or federal sectors will alter the process substantially for many buyers.

There are however, several steps that most selection processes will go through. Like with any large scale investment, the buyer wants to overcome as many information barriers as possible. With any economic transaction, there is often an information failure problem to overcome, in order to maximise the expected future supplier derived benefit and reduce cost. How can a buyer reduce supplier uncertainty?

There are several basic steps to follow:

1. Understand the current and future business requirements and pain points
2. Overlay existing approaches and orthogonal technologies
3. Leverage independent research such as market analysis, peer reviews and technology integrator reports and consultations
4. Engage request for information, request for proposal and proof of concept processes to understand competitive offerings
5. Perform specific due diligence on particular vendors

Whilst that list is not exhaustive, it provides a set of basic building blocks that can help reduce risk when it comes to supplier choice. The buyer needs to be in a solid position with respect to understanding of their own needs.

Future Business Requirements

> *Chapters 5* and *6* aimed to provide the mechanics that help to understand the current internal requirements landscape. It is vitality important to understand what direction the CIAM platform will head towards. If a direction and set of strategic assumptions are not created, it is highly likely that the prospective supplier will heavily influence

direction. This often results in the buyer creating a set of "wants" instead of a set of "needs". Those "wants" are often then heavily tied to a supplier's specific feature set, allowing competitive comparison to become difficult. It is also important to think of the future requirements, not just today's.

Existing Approaches

Analysis of existing approaches to providing CIAM services should be both an inside-out and outside-in process. It is highly likely that even in a "greenfield" deployment, they will be custom and shadow systems delivering some level of capability. Perhaps existing vendor supplied software being used out of pattern, custom applications or open source tooling could already be providing a level of capability. From an outside-in perspective, which competitors are delivering the types of functionality the new CIAM platform will seek to solve? It is very likely the business requirements identified in *chapters 5* and *6* are likely to be being driven from a market perspective, with competitors already delivering similar capabilities. Did they develop in house, use a commercial product or customisable consultancy package?

Market Research

Clearly if the procurement of commercial software and services is necessary, performing some sort of market analysis is essential. There are numerous market analysis organisations, which can often be overwhelming. This process can really be broken down into two camps: market intelligence and supplier intelligence. Understanding the market may well require the procurement of dedicated report materials that showcase the history, main suppliers, trends, market size, technology overview and so on. The likes of Gartner and Forrester research firms can provide such material. The output of that market background is likely to produce a list of potential suppliers. We covered many of these in *chapter 2*. At this point it is worth performing vendor specific research. Downloading case studies, data sheets, watching YouTube demonstrations and so on. Understand vendor specific terminology versus industry standard terms and standards. Highlight vendor specific concepts or approaches–are they proprietary and likely to cause vendor lock in, or providing real visionary thought?

Formal Engagement

The formal vendor engagement process is likely to contain several different levels of interaction. This could include requests for information, formal proposals, pitches, demo's and proof of concepts. It is important to be consistent, clear and focused during this process. Standardization of this is critical, not only to provide vendor clarity and impartiality, but also to help analyse competitive differences in feature set and delivery. Vendor supply costs will clearly be different and there is a reason for this: vendors are likely offering different functionality and in turn value and it is important to be able to baseline and compare those differences.

Deep Dive Due Diligence

When it comes to pricing and contract negotiation, the greater the level of due diligence that has been performed, the better position the buy side decision maker will be in. This level of due diligence could be time consuming and may require consultants and experts in certain fields and suppliers. It is likely this will only be applied to one or 2 shortlisted suppliers, where negotiations are taking place. Due diligence should try to help answer supplier questions such as:

- Are they expanding/shrinking their market share?
- Are they hiring/firing?
- What references applicable to the known requirements exist?
- What peer reviews are available?
- Have they received funding recently?
- If a public company, what information is in their most recent financial reports?
- What key messages are their social accounts promoting?
- What does their technology roadmap look like?

The vendor selection process is likely to take months not weeks, albeit the actual timeline will be specific to any business or project requirements. Don't underestimate how long this process can take. If engaging multiple vendors, there will be differences in how the suppliers operate, how and when they will provide data, even if they have been provided with a timeline of events.

Analysis of the response data and individual research will also take some considerable time. Information needs to be collated, centralised and documented in a repeatable and comparable way that allows for simple scoring and discussion.

Sample RFP

The request for proposal will likely be a critical tool in helping to downgrade and eventually select a supplier. The purpose of the RFP is to help extract critical supplier information in a simple, structured and comparable fashion, whilst being fair and transparent to the potential supplier.

The Why

> The main introductory part of the RFP should contain a key section describing the need for the RFP, the project aims and the high level background that resulted in the RFP being issued. What is the buyer trying to achieve? Why is this important to them and why is it important now? Why is it time critical? What is the impact to the buyer or not deploying this solution in a timely fashion? This

general positioning can really help suppliers understand the north star of the buyer and the real underpinnings of their needs, not just the "nice to haves".

Company & Technical Background

Even if the buyer is from a multinational famous brand or a niche startup, it is essential the supplier has a good understanding of the company history, structure and purpose as well as the existing technical architecture and operations that are in place. This may seem like the mundane details for the buyer, but the supplier will find this information incredibly useful, from both a solutions design and negotiations perspective, but also a technical integration standpoint too. By understanding how the organisation is structured and operating, the buyer can improve their system integration approaches, service level agreements and contractual design. It might also be prudent, where possible, for the buyer to describe why certain technical architecture decisions were made and how they were implemented. For example, the selection of a cloud based database was not possible due to external regulatory requirements, or the fact that there is an open source first approach due to extensive customisation requirements.

Proposal Guidance & Timeline

Getting suppliers to respond to a proposal can at times be difficult. The time commitment from the supplier will be significant and depending on the number of vendors being compared, may result in a very high chance the effort will be for nothing. The proposal is likely to contain various different sections regarding what information the supplier needs to provide–from their own background, financial data, case studies, technical descriptions, support models and so on. How that information needs to be presented needs to be clearly articulated. Will the responses be made into a pre-packaged spreadsheet? Will PDFs do? How will case studies be collected and analysed? Will that require interviews with the supplier's references? If the supplier is being asked to perform demonstrations, are they to be canned and recorded, or live via a conference call? Cleary instructions including data format, word count and what is acceptable (links to documents, yes) and what is not (promises and comments on future roadmaps, no) will be needed.

Provide an opportunity for the supplier to ask questions, query the process and raise any concerns they have regarding the information they have been provided. It is typical to provide a window of consultation to allow suppliers to consume the proposal and respond with a written list of queries. It is also quite common for each supplier to in turn see other suppliers queries for full transparency.

Finally a timeline should also be included. Whilst not always accurate, they do at least show a procedural set of steps that the buyer is working towards. Invariably that timeline may fall short (more vendors respond requiring longer analysis, vendor's ask for extensions, key stakeholders are unavailable and so on), but a timeline shows a commitment of sorts and that encourages vendors to partner and contribute to the process.

Requirements (Functional)

This section should outline the main requirements that are needed to service the CIAM platform. We covered a high level set of requirements in chapter 3 as well as in the chapter 4 CIAM lifecycle. This will contain a list of specific features that are needed. Vendors are likely to claim they can perform every feature, so aim to identify items that perhaps are not provided out of the box, or require customisation. Probe for examples, documentation links and experience based responses that show that a vendor has delivered a piece of functionality previously.

It can often be useful to break this section down into the various different groups of functionality such as registration, authentication, data sharing, MFA, adaptive access, marketing integration and so on. Keep this section succinct and don't simply create a long list of "nice to haves" based on market reports. Focus on what is needed immediately, what will be needed for the next 24-36 month roadmap and attempt to identify where certain features seem like stretch goals or bespoke customisations.

Requirements (Non-Functional)

Non-functional requirements should follow the same format as the functional. Be succinct, descriptive and ask for the "how do you", rather than the "can you do...". Capacity, throughput, availability and security style questions can nearly also result in affirmative responses from the supplier, but it is important to again understand where the supplier has fulfilled those requirements previously. Ask for specifics. For example, "How do you provide fault tolerance and data replication between EMEA and North America", rather than "Does your solution support fault tolerance?". Closed questions may seem a good choice for normalisation and vendor comparison, but ironically it may turn out the opposite, if all vendors respond affirmatively, it can become incredibly difficult to identify weakness.

Support & Services

Platforms, software and development kits don't come in isolation. They need integrating, installing and customizing in order to create the appropriate value the buyer is looking for. What services does the vendor provide? Can they augment existing operational teams with consultants, trainers, business analysts and developers? Do they have partnerships with system integrators who perform the integration work on their behalf? If so ask for references. Are the integrators experienced with your combination of functional, non-functional and integration requirements? Does the system integrator provide near-shore or off-shore delivery? Are these of concern in the buy side operational model?

Support is more likely to come directly from the vendor, so identify the levels of support available and any advertised problem response and resolution times. What sort of support models are available? Ticketing systems, remote dial in, 24 x 7 around the globe support, or purely office hours in certain regions?

Inquire about service level agreements if the vendor is delivering via a SaaS or PaaS model and how things like maintenance, upgrades and security patching is handled.

Pricing

What will all this cost? Clearly complex middleware and platform focused software and services is firstly, not cheap and secondly not a one-size-fits-all process. Comparing different vendors based on functionality can be challenging, but overlay on top of that, that each vendor is likely to provide different cost values, structures and payment terms. Ask suppliers to be entirely clear regarding overall costs–including software licenses, support, integration and so on. Is a subscription charged per year available, or a perpetual license that provides lifetime access? Are licensing costs calculated on a per user basis, or per API call? How does the vendor articulate what a user actually is? Is a user an entry in a directory, and if so is the level of user activity important?

Clearly the more functionality the buyer is willing to buy, the bigger the expected discount. The same for user volume and term of contract. Larger deal size, should result in larger discounts. Be cognizant of when the suppliers end or quarter or end of fiscal year ends, as this could help drive improved terms.

When looking at feature roadmaps of both the buy side and supplier side, be aware of changes to future pricing and costs. The first year may seem "cheap" but costs may ramp substantially based on the number of increased user registrations or required feature extensions.

References

One last point regarding the RFP process and that is on references. References, case studies, peer reviews and expert testimonials are invaluable. The information generated by the RFP process must also be leveraged against speaking with trusted professionals who have experience with working alongside the prospective supplier. References should be a part of the RFP response and access to them should ideally be available without the vendor present. Where possible leverage impartial system integrators or partners who have industry experience of the vendor. Perhaps they have implemented the technology, know employees, or have worked there previously. The Gartner research firm provides a free "Peer Insights"[147] service via their website, which allows quick research and comparison of key software suppliers based on implementation approaches and feedback. Other analyst firms provide similar services (for a cost) but they are worth investigating.

PoC Design

The proof of concept process is a likely extension of the RFP. It would be typical to go through an RFP process with up to 10 vendors, albeit many start with less. The downgrade process is likely to result in perhaps 3 suppliers who will be eligible and willing to go to the next stage of the process, which is some sort of technology proof, pilot or proof of concept.

A PoC is not a trivial process. It will take a large

147https://www.gartner.com/reviews/home

commitment from both the buy side and supply side. PoC scenarios, testing data and systems, infrastructure (either virtual, cloud or other), access to personnel as well as scoring, demo's and feedback all take up valuable time and resources. Preparation work will be significant and the PoC itself could last anywhere between a week to a month.

The appetite for the PoC will of course be directly linked to the cost of winning the proposed piece of work. If the overall cost is $50,000, a month long PoC with an experienced consultant is unlikely to seem attractive to a vendor.

There are several alternatives to the classic PoC process, such as prepared demo's, cloud play grounds and workshops but whichever is chosen, the understanding of using or seeing close at hand a vendor solution provides invaluable insight.

Aims of the PoC

> The end goal of a PoC is to understand the technical fit of the supplier. Are the use cases easily integrated? Is the tooling, user interfaces and documentation stable and mature? Are the staff competent and experienced? What is the working manner of the supplier? Are they a good culture fit for the buy side operational teams and able to integrate effectively?
>
> Like the RFP process, it is important to be very clear

surrounding the buyer expectations regarding the PoC. Describe scenarios succinctly, which should cover any specific demonstration steps or successful exit criteria that must be achieved. Scoring and pointing systems should be transparent and well documented.

From a scenario perspective, pick use cases that are pertinent to the value associated with the CIAM project, not use cases you think the supplier will either excel at or struggle with. Use data or systems that are specific to the buy side environment. Perhaps supply anonymised yet product-like data sets, APIs, target applications, user interface requirements and so on.

Practical Steps

Limit the number of vendors in the PoC process. A minimum of 2, a maximum of three. Any more than three and the chances are the RFP process needs expanding in order to provide better differentiation between chosen suppliers. Any fewer than 2 and the buy side competitive position can become compromised and the vendor will have a negotiation advantage when it comes to pricing and contracts. Leverage formal scoring systems and include as many diversified use cases possible, that cover the practical aspects of the implementation. Don't focus on the most cutting edge use cases if they only account for 5% of the feature roadmap, when in fact integration with an unusual legacy database is likely the first step in any production deployment. Be honest with feedback. If something is working tell the vendor. If on day 3 the process, culture, feedback or technology is not a good fit, be clear on that too. Vendors will appreciate the transparency.

Not all PoC's are equal. Not only are the costs significant, but many supplier delivery models may be different too. Some may be SaaS, PaaS, open source, consultancy lead or entirely self service. Try to identify what the most consistent and most effective approach could be. It may well be a 2 day workshop with each vendor where they design on whiteboards any potential solution to specific use cases, right through to an actual pilot that is deployed in the buy side data centres.

Prepared Demonstration

Whilst not a full PoC, a prepared demonstration, based on key scenarios the buyer wants to see integrated, can provide useful context surrounding how the supplier works and how complex the user interfaces, tooling, libraries and documentation are. It also provides insights into how the supplier works. "Canned" demos on generic use cases provide limited insight, but specifically prepared demos on buy side scenarios can be cost effective and useful exercises. How the demos are built is also a useful exercise in itself. It is not uncommon for vendors to be asked to come onsite to the prospective customer and spend 2-3 days building the demo in front of them. The actual finished demo may only account for 10% of the overall scoring, whereas the "working out" may well be more useful for the buy side team to understand the tooling, challenges, logs and documentation available.

DIY

Allowing the buy side to do the PoC themselves is often another trojan horse approach in evaluating the prospective supplier. Whether the supplier is providing a cloud based SaaS or an open source set of libraries and APIs, having the buy side download, install or integrate themselves can prove a useful smoke test regarding capability, culture and "feel" for integration. Self-service approaches like this also help so show buy side commitment to the suppliers. By spending 1 or 2 weeks understanding how a supplier's technology works, shows a need to understand and a willingness to learn new approaches and tooling. The buy side will clearly have a nuanced understanding of their own environment which can make use case integration easier from one perspective, if the supplier is able to provide technical support and counselling to get the best out of the supplier materials.

Full PoC

The most time demanding and costly approach is to

perform a pull PoC within the customers ecosystem. If the delivery is on prem, this will require integration to existing private cloud, datacentres or virtualisation environments in test and pre-prod stages. Data sets will be from as near production ready systems as possible and integrations using actual if only test APIs. This by far will be the most time consuming, not least as many buy side ecosystems, if not production-like will require change control and infrastructure spin-up processes. Whilst a lot of that could be performed in advance, it is likely delays will be faced with unforeseen issues when done for real. Whilst this may mirror the real production environment, the practical aspects of providing access could be too high.

If such a level of due diligence is required, it may well result in the PoC being termed a pilot with a successful outcome guaranteeing a procurement of at least the services expended by the service provider. The outcome of the process will provide a lasting and detailed integration experience for the buy side. This is especially true where a pure cloud supplier is being chosen, the cloud deployment can simply be "upgraded" to a production level of support.

Whatever PoC approach is chosen, where possible attempt to run simultaneous vendor integrations. If not, the ordering of vendor integration could well help or hinder their outcome, with the buy side becoming more experienced regarding their own integrations once they see a vendor attempt to deliver what is being asked.

Typically the first vendor is compared to the written use cases and theoretical requirements, whereas the last vendor is often compared to the previous one relatively. That can have a fundamental impact on scoring and selection.

Summary
Vendor and supplier selection can be a tricky and time consuming process. A successful selection from both the buy side and supply side, comes about from thorough preparation, a solid understanding of the business requirements, stakeholder commitment and transparent dialogue with all suppliers involved.

CHAPTER 9

Measuring Success

We are coming to the end of our journey into the world of CIAM requirements and design. In this chapter, we will conclude the book by taking a look at how to measure the success of a CIAM implementation, why measuring success is important and discuss some examples of what can be measured.

Why Metrics Matter

The executive leadership team in any organisation is driven by data which in turn helps provide business intelligence (BI). That BI helps teams make more informed decisions regarding investment, structure and go to market strategy.

KPIs or key performance indicators are the components that feed into that overarching intelligence programme. The likes of cyber security and identity and access management tooling and solutions are often measured in order to identify their impact on the greater business aims.

For example, if a business objective is to improve net promoter scores (NPS), and have more existing customers recommend the business or service to others, the factors that influence that NPS value could be related to the level of trust the customer has in the business. How could trust hamper the KPI of increasing the NPS? Well if the organisation is involved in a data breach which is badly received in the media, or perhaps isn't seen to handle PII processing very well, those technical level controls could roll up into having a negative impact on the bigger business object. That is a very simplified example, but if the linking of tooling and solutions is important to the overall success of the business, it is important to be able measure the granular level components.

Many see measurement of any sort, as interfering with the overall task of "getting the job done". Timesheets, costings, baselining and so on, are often seen as a management and reporting jobs and not the purview of the subject matter expert upholding a control or designing a process.

However, metrics of all types perform a two fold function: not only do they provide a mechanism for other (especially non technical) community members to understand the direction of travel or progress being made, but they also allow a focus on improvement, which benefits all parts of the work hierarchy. If something can be measured it can be improved.

Metrics can come in a few different flavours too. The analyst firm Gartner describe this quite well in their paper "Demonstrate Control Over User Access With IAM Effectiveness Metrics"[148]. Whilst this really focuses on internal identity and access management, the metric types can be broken down in three distinct camps: metrics for *coverage*, metrics for *effectiveness* and metrics for *performance*.

148https://www.gartner.com/document/3863776 (subscription required)

Coverage

Coverage is for those investing in identity and looking for the high level coarse grained view of the world. If we translate this to the CIAM space, that would be looking at how identity services are perhaps being used to capture and acquire new service users or increase conversion during a digital supermarket transaction.

Performance

Performance metrics are generally the most obvious to define and capture. They typically look at the speed, volume, throughput and rate style measurements. How many users can be logged in during a peak hour run through on the CIAM platform, or how many password resets a minute can be handled? The main use for performance metrics is really in being able to look at a long tail of data and identify trends, peaks, and patterns.

Effectiveness

Effectiveness metrics are really an extension of some performance related analysis, but with the addition of context. That context may pertain to industry or competitor comparisons, or to a line with business growth objectives or change. For example if a performance metric exists regarding the timing of logins relating to the setup of MFA for risky transactions, perhaps effectiveness is focused upon high risk transaction reduction from a fraud analytics standpoint, or perhaps how switching MFA modal results in a 15% time reduction to perform the transaction.

Controls or Outcomes?

One other point to consider when it comes to designing metrics is the flow between controls and outcomes. Controls tend to be quite low level - often feature related, with outcomes being a much more pragmatic and reportable characteristic. For example a control metric could be to measure the rollout of a MFA flow for newly registered users to the CIAM platform. The higher the number of users enrolled to use MFA, the better the metric result. An outcome based approach could be instead to focus upon how the number of high risk events were identified and blocked, resulting in a reduced risk of data breach. Even if the MFA metric is measured and in turn increased, the overall risk posture of the business may not be altered which in turn has limited impact on global objectives.

As with all metrics, it is important to identify what really "tips the needle" when it comes to business objectives. CIAM is there to support business activity so it is important to assign metrics that can relate to having an impact (positively and negatively) to business outcomes.

Regardless of what type of metric has been designed, it is important to return that value calculation back to the return on investment or value to the business. What is this piece of functionality, software or outcome attempting to achieve? How can success be defined and in turn measured?

If the component being measured were deemed to increase to a point of defined "success", what does that mean to the business? Was a monetary value saved? Were more customers attracted to the service? Did the existing customers spend more? Were compliance fines reduced?

If the metric can not be articulated into a chain of hierarchy like the *objectives*, *strategies* and *tactics* we described back in *chapter 1*, it is likely it may need redesigning.

Success Samples

Let us focus a little on some concrete examples of metrics specifically tied to CIAM platform and service deployments.

User Acquisition

As with all metrics, it is important to cover the different CIAM stakeholders, and the CMO is likely very interested in the volume and turnover or new user activity. A main driver of many CIAM projects is to ultimately increase the adoption of a service and the revenue of the business. User acquisition (either from physical to digital migrations, or net new) is a key part of that process.

Figure 9.1 User acquisition metrics

Coverage	Performance	Effectiveness
Number of net new customers to the service	How many user's authenticate per month/day/hour?	Can the registration process be done without support, across a range of user communities and devices?

Shopping Cart Abandonment

Not all CIAM systems will be servicing ecommerce or retail related functions. However the abandoned shopping cart, where a user has interacted with and made decisions within a service, only to then walk away, is often tied to poor authentication and validation functionality. Improving this part of the user journey will not transform a business selling bad products, it will certainly inhibit a business form selling a good product if it's done badly.

Figure 9.2 Shopping cart abandonment metrics

Coverage	Performance	Effectiveness
User transaction completion rate	How long does a OTP	Does the time it takes to

	authentication event take versus FIDO2?	perform an MFA event correlate with customer walk away before payment?

Agent Assisted Support

All identity platforms, whether they are internal or external focused, will have some sort of agent assisted support process - aka the "helpdesk". The helpdesk can be a costly and complex centre, with logical and technical links to many other parts of the business and associated technology. The main cost of course is often people and CIO's are keen to design playbooks that allow them to automate many of the repeated interactions as possible, before augmenting with self service.

Figure 9.3 Agent assisted support metrics

Coverage	Performance	Effectiveness
Understand per interaction cost of agent assistance	Capture helpdesk call volumes during user onboarding, proofing, credential reset and lost device	Opportunity cost of delivering a self service process that results in dissatisfied end users that do not refer the service to

		others

Compliance Costs

For many CIAM platforms privacy preservation may be seen as a competitive advantage in the process of treating customers like partners and building and keeping their trust. However, for many CIO's, compliance in the form of external regulation or internal audit, is an omnipresent concern.

Figure 9.4 Compliance cost metrics

Coverage	Performance	Effectiveness
Understand overall compliance support cost	Capture the number of open compliance issues against core GDPR requirements	Does the number of post-audit open issues reduce when leveraging a data discovery and pipeline approach to PII?

Data Breach Reduction

Having "data breach reduction" as a key business objective, is often like an Olympic athlete aiming to "keep fit and healthy" over the course of a season. Whilst true, with some incredibly injury prone athletes aiming for that objective in some years, many organisations will likely already have implicit controls in place that aid the data breach prevention mantra. This can become of increased importance for many CISO's, as soon as consumer data is being held and processed as part of the CIAM platform.

Figure 9.5 Data breach reduction metrics

Coverage	Performance	Effectiveness
Capture share price impact based on brand damage due to data breach	How many failed authorization (403 errors) identified on customer self service platforms?	Does MFA tied to failed authorization reduce bot activity associated with automated data attacks?

Summary

The success of the CIAM platform is not tied to the metrics that are designed, but they will help to provide guidance regarding future investment, technical changes and the alignment to future business goals.

Metrics, like most parts of the CIAM design journey, require stakeholder buy in from across the entire organisation. If done correctly, a CIAM platform will become a foundational part of business transformation, that creates a solid, yet agile platform that allows for evolving growth and improved customer satisfaction.

Final Comments

The previous nine chapters should have taken you on a journey to understand a little more about the vocabulary and purpose of consumer identity and access management.

This was by no means the entire chronicle of what you may encounter designing a solution, choosing a vendor or analysing requirements. It should however, allow your role as an architect, or specialist or information leader, to develop a set of consistent patterns, language and terminology that will help to unite different stakeholders involved in opening up resources, designing new services and developing secure digital relationships with external identities.

Please reach out at https://www.simonmoffatt.com to discuss your progress and comments.